MON

NATSUME SOSEKI

MON
(The Gate)

*Translated from the Japanese
by Francis Mathy*

A PERIGEE BOOK

Perigee Books
are published by
G. P. Putnam's Sons
200 Madison Avenue
New York, New York 10016

UNESCO COLLECTION OF REPRESENTATIVE WORKS
JAPANESE SERIES

This book has been accepted in the
Japanese Literature Translation Series
of the United Nations Educational, Scientific
and Cultural Organization (UNESCO).

Translated from the Japanese *Mon*

Library of Congress Cataloging in Publication Data

Natsume, Sōseki, 1867-1916.
Mon-The gate.

Fiction.
Reprint. Originally published: London : Owen, 1972.
(UNESCO collection of representative works.
Japanese series)
"A Perigee Book."
I. Title: Gate.   II. Series: UNESCO collection of
representative works. Japanese series.
PL812.A8M613   1982   895.6'34   81-15427
ISBN 0-399-50608-X   AACR2

First Perigee printing, 1982
Printed in the United States of America

MON

1

Sosuke had brought a cushion on to the veranda and plopped himself on it, cross-legged, and was now basking in the midafternoon sun. After a time he tossed aside the magazine he held in his hands and stretched himself out full length on his side. It was a beautiful Indian summer day. The rhythmic clip-clop of *geta** in the streets of the hushed town fell pleasantly on his ears. Raising himself up on his elbow, he looked out beyond the eaves of the house at the beautiful, clear sky, blue all over. Viewed from the tiny veranda, it seemed extremely vast. It made quite a difference, he reflected, to be able on an occasional Sunday to gaze leisurely at the sky like this. He looked squint-eyed directly into the sun, but only for a moment. The light was too blinding, and so he turned on his other side till he faced the *shoji* behind which his wife, Oyone, was at work sewing.

'What wonderful weather!'

'Yes.' She added nothing more. Since Sosuke too was not eager, seemingly, to start a conversation, they fell back into silence. After a time it was Oyone who spoke.

'Why don't you go for a walk?'

Sosuke grunted noncommittally and did not move.

Several minutes later when she chanced to look out of the window of the *shoji* onto the veranda, Oyone saw that her husband was asleep. He had both knees pulled up close to him, shrimp-like, and his black head was buried in his folded arms, face completely invisible.

* Definitions of Japanese terms are given in the glossary on page 215.

'If you go to sleep there, you're sure to catch cold,' she cautioned. Her speech was almost that of a native Tokyoite, but not quite. It had the inflections common to graduates of girls' academies all over Japan.

Sosuke opened his eyes but did not raise his head. 'It's all right. I won't fall asleep,' he answered in a low voice.

All fell still again. A passing *jinrikisha* rang its bell two or three times. A cock crowed in the distance. The sounds reached Sosuke without his really listening to them, as he basked in the warm sunbeams that pierced through the weave of his newly-made kimono and penetrated to the bone.

Suddenly, as if recalling something, he called out to his wife, 'Oyone, how do you write the character for *kin* in *kinrai*?'

Oyone showed no surprise that he should have forgotten how to write this simple character, nor did she laugh the shrill laugh peculiar to young women.

'It's the character for *oo* in *oomi*,' she replied.

'But that's what I can't remember — the character for the *oo* of *oomi*.'

She half opened the *shoji* and drew the character for *kin* on the veranda floor with her long ruler, saying only 'It's this.' The point of her ruler rested where it was at the end of the last stroke of the character as she stood for a moment gazing at the transparent sky.

'Yes, of course,' said Sosuke, without looking up at her. This lapse of memory did not strike him as particularly humorous and he did not laugh. Oyone too passed the incident off casually.

'This is really fine weather.' She spoke half to herself. She returned to her work, leaving the doors to the veranda open.

Sosuke lifted his head slightly from his arms and said, 'Characters are funny things, aren't they?' For the first time he raised his eyes to his wife's face.

'Why?'

6

'When you begin to doubt how to write even the simplest character, you get completely confused. The other day too I had a hard time recalling the character for the *kon* of *konnichi*. I wrote it down on paper and looked at it. Something seemed wrong. And the longer I looked, the less like *kon* it seemed. Haven't you ever had that experience?'

'No, certainly not.'

'Then it's only me.'

'I think something's wrong with you.'

'I suppose I've got a pretty bad case of nerves.'

'Yes, I think so too,' she agreed, looking into his face.

Finally he rose. He stepped over her sewing box and thread, walked through the *chanoma* where she was working and opened the doors to the next room, which was the parlour. Since the southern exposure was blocked off by the front vestibule, the *shoji* at the other end of the room appeared indistinct to his eyes, adjusted as they were to the broad sunlight. He opened these too and stepped onto the eastern veranda. Here a high cliff, which seemed to press down upon the eaves of the house, rose from beside the veranda, so that even the morning sun, which should have come streaming in, could not easily disperse the shadows. Grass was planted on the slope, but there were no stones to hold the bank in place, so that there was always fear of a landslide. Strangely enough, none had ever occurred. Perhaps for that reason the landlord had left it untouched for so long. The grocer, who had lived in the neighbourhood for some twenty years, had explained at the kitchen door one day that the slope had once been covered with a bamboo thicket and that when the trees had been cut down the roots had been left in place. The soil was thus firmer than one might expect. Sosuke's response had been that if the roots had remained in place, why hadn't a new crop of trees flourished? The grocer had answered that once you cut down trees like this, they do not easily grow back. But that, in any case, the embankment was firm, and whatever happened it would not come crashing down on them. He had spoken with great assurance, as if the cliff were his responsibility, and then had taken his departure.

The embankment displayed nothing of autumn colour. The only indication of autumn was the absence of the smell of fresh grass and the dishevelled, ragged appearance of the slope. Neither the *susuki* nor the *tsuta* nor any of the other lovely grasses of autumn were to be seen. Instead, two stalks of *moso* bamboo rose abruptly at the middle of the slope and another three near the top, remnants of a former time. These were slightly tinged with gold, and gave the impression that if one stood directly behind them as they were struck by the sun, the warmth of autumn would come into view just over the cliff. Since Sosuke always left the house in the early morning and didn't return until after four, he seldom had the leisure to view the top of the cliff at this time of day with the sun high in the sky. He came out of the dark toilet and washed his hands. As he let the water run over his fingers, he happened to look up beyond the eaves of the house and he recalled the bamboo. At the top of some of the bamboo stalks he saw a rich growth of leaves, looking very much like the stubble of a monk's close-shaven head. The leaves, folded one upon the other, appeared to be entranced by the autumn sun as they gazed heavily downwards in complete silence, not a single one stirring.

Sosuke closed the *shoji*, returned to the parlour, and squatted down before the low table. The room could be called a parlour only because it was where they received their guests. It was really more of a study or a little sitting-room. On the northern side of the room was the *tokonoma*, in which hung a very odd token scroll, with a rather pathetic flower vase, the colour of burnt amber, before it. There were no pictures on the walls, only two bent brass nails that caught the sunlight. There was also a bookcase

8

with glass doors, but with nothing inside of sufficient interest to catch the eye.

Sosuke opened the drawers of the table, which was gilded in gold and silver, and began to rummage through them for something. Not finding what he was looking for, he closed them with a bang. Then he opened the lid of his inkstone case and began to write a letter. He finished the letter, sealed it, and paused in thought for a moment. Then he turned to his wife in the next room and asked,

'What was Aunt Saeki's address in Naka roku bancho?'

'Wasn't it number twenty-five?' Oyone replied. Sosuke wrote it on the envelope.

'A letter won't do. You've got to go and see her.'

'At any rate, let's try a letter first, even if it's useless. If that fails, I'll go and have a talk with her.' He spoke emphatically, and when his wife did not reply, he added, 'That ought to be good enough, don't you think?'

Oyone did not seem sure enough of her opinion to contradict him and she did not press her objection. Sosuke, letter in hand, stepped at once from the parlour into the vestibule, then outside. Oyone left her place only when she heard him leaving the house. She went to the entrance to see him off.

'I'm going for a short walk.'

'Please do,' Oyone answered smiling.

Half an hour later Oyone heard the front door open. She put aside her sewing and went out along the veranda to the vestibule, expecting to see her husband back. Instead it was his younger brother, Koroku, school cap on his head and a long, black woollen mantle that reached almost to the floor about his shoulders.

'It's hot,' he said, as he unfastened the mantle.

'Isn't that too much . . . a heavy thing like that in this fine weather?'

'I thought it would get cold when the sun went down,' Koroku explained. He followed his sister-in-law into the

9

next room. Seeing the kimono she was working on, he commented, 'I see you're as busy as ever,' and sat down in front of the charcoal brazier. Oyone put away her sewing and sat opposite him. She took the tea-kettle off the brazier and began to put in more charcoal.

'Please don't bother about tea.'

'You don't care for tea? Then how about some cake?' Oyone asked laughing.

'Do you have any in the house?'

'No, I don't,' she answered frankly, and then, remembering something, 'Just a second. There may be some after all.' She rose quickly, pushing aside the charcoal scuttle which was in the way. She opened the door of a little cupboard and began searching through it, her back turned towards Koroku, who kept his eyes on her. She took so long that he finally interrupted her.

'Never mind about the cake. Tell me where I can find my brother.'

'Your brother has just. . . .' Oyone began to answer without turning around, continuing her search in the cupboard. Finally she slammed the doors shut. 'It's no use. Your brother must have finished it off.' She returned to the brazier.

'That's all right. You can treat me to dinner instead.'

'Fine, I'll do that.' Looking at the wall clock, she saw that it was almost four. She counted the hours to dinner: 'Four, five, six o'clock.' Koroku looked at her without speaking. He really wasn't very excited about the dinner invitation.

'Oyone, did my brother go to see Aunt Saeki?' he asked.

'He's been thinking of going for a long time, but he leaves the house early and returns late. When he gets back, he's so tired that it's a great effort even to go out to the bath. So don't be hard on him.'

'I know how busy he is, but until I get this thing settled, it's so much on my mind that I can't get down to serious study.' As he said this, he took up the brass tongs and began to write in the ashes with them. Oyone watched the moving tips of the tongs.

'But at least he's written a letter,' she said as if to console him.

'What did the letter say?'

'I didn't read it. But I'm sure it was about that matter. He'll be back soon. You can ask him yourself. But you can be sure. . . .'

'If he wrote to Aunt Saeki, it must have been about that.'

'Yes, I'm sure he sent her a letter. In fact, he just went out to post it.'

Koroku did not care to listen further to his sister-in-law's words, spoken half by way of apology, half in order to console him. He thought that if his brother had the time for a walk, he could just as well have gone to see Mrs Saeki, instead of only sending her a letter. He was not in a very good mood. He stepped into the parlour and took a red-bound foreign book out of the bookcase and began to flip through the pages.

II

Sosuke walked to the corner, stopped at a shop to buy some cigarettes and a postage stamp for his letter, then posted the letter in a nearby box. Not feeling like retracing his steps immediately, he kept on walking at a leisurely pace, the smoke from his cigarette trailing off in the autumn air. Before he knew it, he had walked some distance. The sights and sounds of Tokyo made a strong impression on him today. Then suddenly he felt like going home and treating himself to a Sunday nap. All the year round he breathed the air of Tokyo. Daily he rode on the streetcar to and from work, passing morning and evening through the bustling streets. But he was always so fatigued in mind and body that he travelled in a daze, completely unaware of his surroundings. Recently he had even lost consciousness of the fact that he was living in the midst of so much activity. He was so busy usually that he did not have time to think about it, but when the seventh day of the week came round, the day of holiday, and he had a chance to rest and compose himself, he would suddenly become aware of the nervous tension of his daily life. When he reflected that though he lived in the heart of Tokyo, he had never really taken a good look at the city, a strange melancholy would come over him.

At such times he would dash into the streets, and if he happened to have money in his pocket, he would even think of exploring the pleasures of the big city. But his melancholy was never so deep as to precipitate an ill-considered action, and before he did anything impulsively, he would reconsider and end up laughing at his foolishness. Besides, the usual condition of his wallet counselled against rashness, and rather than strain his ingenuity for a means of realizing his whim, he found it more pleasant to stroll leisurely home, hands in pockets. And so by a simple walk through the city or window shopping in an arcade his melancholy would be alleviated until the following Sunday.

Today too he decided to see a little of the city and so he boarded a streetcar. Despite the wonderful weather, there were fewer passengers than usual and he found the ride more pleasant than he had ever known it. Better still, the passengers all had an air of serenity; each one looked composed and relaxed. As he sat down, he thought of the daily struggle for seats on the car for Marunouchi that he boarded at the same time each morning, every passenger for himself as he tried to push ahead of the others. No travelling companions, he reflected, were as boorish as those who rode the streetcar during the rush hours. He had never been able to detect any sign of human warmth in the passengers hanging on to the straps or sitting on the velvet cushions.

In his disgust he too became like a machine, impersonally lining up his knees with theirs when he sat or brushing shoulders with them when he stood, sharing the same car until his stop and then just as impersonally getting off.

Opposite him was an elderly woman with a girl of eight or so, probably her granddaughter. She had her mouth to the child's ear and was saying something to her. Near them another woman of about thirty, a shopkeeper perhaps, looked on with warm interest, and then began to engage the little girl in conversation, asking her name and age, and so forth. Sosuke felt as if he had stepped into another world.

Overhead, filling every available space, hung a variety of framed advertisements. Ordinarily these escaped his notice completely, but now for no particular reason he began to read them one by one. 'It's easy if you leave the moving to us,' advised the first, the slogan of a removals firm. On the next, arranged in consecutive lines, were the following phrases:

IF YOU'RE LOOKING FOR ECONOMY
IF YOU'RE WORRIED ABOUT SANITATION
IF YOU'RE AFRAID OF ACCIDENTAL FIRE

Then at the bottom: 'Use a gas burner'. Alongside the words was a drawing of a gas burner with a flame shooting out from it. The third advertisement was for a popular adaptation of a novel by Tolstoy, the current presentation of a Tokyo dramatic group, white letters on a red background.

In about ten minutes Sosuke had read each of the advertisements at least three times, not overlooking a single character. He was not moved to go to see or to buy the products advertised, but it was no small satisfaction just to have these advertisements impressed clearly in his head, to have had the leisure to peruse each one and understand thoroughly what it said. His present life was such that only on Sunday could he boast of this leisure. On other days his comings and goings were anything but relaxed.

He got off the streetcar at Surugadai. As he stepped down, his eye was caught by an attractive arrangement of Western books in a shop window immediately to the right of him. He stood for a while in front of it, looking at the lively gold lettering on cloth of all colours and designs. He understood their titles, of course, but he had not the slightest desire to handle the books or leaf through them. At one time he had been unable to pass a bookshop without entering, and once inside he always found something he wanted. But that was long ago, part of a life that had passed forever. A book entitled *The History of Gambling*, in the centre of the display, was very beautifully bound and made a vivid impression on him.

Sosuke, a smile on his lips, crossed to the other side of the street and looked into a jeweller's where all kinds of gold watches and chains were on display. He was content to admire their colour and shape and had not the slightest desire to own one. All the same, he scanned each price tag and was surprised to see that gold watches were so inexpensive.

He stopped for a second in front of an umbrella shop, and then before a Western-style haberdashery. His eye was caught by a stylish cravat displayed next to a silk hat. It was much nicer than the one he wore every day and he decided to go in and ask the price. He was already halfway in when he thought better of it. After all, what could be gained by appearing at work the next day in a new cravat. He felt suddenly repelled at the very idea of spending money for such a purpose, and he strolled on. He stood next in front of a tailor's, reading the names of the different kinds of weaves, names that had been unfamiliar to him until this moment. Next door to this was the Tokyo branch shop of a famous Kyoto fashion house. He paused for a long time, hat brim thrust up against the show window, ad-

14

miring the delicate embroidery of the women's scarves displayed there. There was one particularly elegant scarf that he thought would look nice on his wife. The thought of buying it and taking it back to her flashed through his mind, but was followed immediately by the reflection that such a gesture would have been fine five or six years earlier but was meaningless now. It had been a good idea, but he put it out of his mind. With a bitter smile on his face he pulled himself away from the window and moved on. He was overcome now by a feeling of futility and was no longer interested in observing either the people or the shops that he passed.

His attention was caught once more by a large newsagent's on the corner, in front of which the latest publications were advertised in large characters. Some of the advertisements consisted of pictures tacked on to a narrow slatted frame; others were long painted boards with pictures arranged to form various designs. He read each one thoroughly. He had come across some of the authors and titles before in newspaper advertisements, while others were completely unfamiliar to him.

Around the corner from this shop a man of about thirty, wearing a derby hat and looking strangely contented as he sat cross-legged on the ground, was selling giant balloons. Blown up, the balloons took the shape of a fat *dharma*. Sosuke was amused to see that the eyes and mouth had been drawn in with charcoal. Once blown up, they remained that way indefinitely and they would balance nicely on the palm of the hand or even on a fingertip. If you stuck something like a toothpick into the aperture at the bottom, the balloon quickly deflated.

A large crowd of people passed by on the busy street but no one paid any attention to the man in the derby or to his balloons. Seemingly unperturbed by the indifference of the passers-by and even unaware of what was going on about him, he continued to sit there cross-legged at the corner of the busy intersection, blowing up his balloons and calling out 'Buy a balloon for the kiddies.' Sosuke took out a few small coins and bought a balloon. The man deflated it for him and he thrust it into his pocket. He decided to go to a clean barber's for a haircut, but before he could find one that suited him, he noticed that the sun was already low in the sky, and so he caught the next streetcar for home. By the time the car reached the end of the line and Sosuke handed his ticket to the driver, the sky had begun to lose colour and black shadows were already menacing the dank streets. The metal hand support which he gripped as he got off the bus was cold to the touch.

The other passengers who got off with him walked away quickly and purposefully in various directions. Looking down the street Sosuke saw what seemed like thin, white smoke circling about in the air between the eaves and the roofs of the houses on both sides. He too walked off hurriedly in the direction of a grove of trees. He felt somewhat sad and let down now that the Sunday and the pleasant weather were at an end. Tomorrow he would have to plunge once more into another week of frenzied activity. He regretted that he would have to wait a full week for another half-day like this, and the remaining six days of exhausting work with no mental relaxation struck him all of a sudden as extremely cheerless. As he walked along, he imagined the scene of the following days: the big, dark office with too few windows, where the sun hardly entered; the face of the colleague who sat next to him; the voice of his boss calling, 'Nonaka, a moment please!'

He passed Uokatsu, the fishmonger, and five or six houses beyond this he turned off into a narrow alley blocked at the other end by a high cliff. To right and left were four or five houses in the same style. Until quite recently there had been mixed in with them an old-fashioned, melancholy house, where behind a scraggly hedge of cryptomeria an old widow was said to be living.

16

But the man who lived on the top of the cliff, Sakai, had bought the place, torn down the thatched roof, uprooted the cryptomeria hedge, and rebuilt the house to look like all the others. Sosuke's house was the last on the left, immediately at the foot of the cliff. It was somewhat dark and gloomy, but since it was the one farthest from the street, it had the advantage of being quiet. It was this that had led Sosuke and Oyone, upon careful consideration, to choose it in preference to the others.

Since the precious Sunday, coming round only once in seven days, was already on its way out, Sosuke hurried to the entrance of the house, planning to go quickly to the public bath, and, if there were time, to get a haircut, then have a leisurely evening meal. From the kitchen came the sound of dishes. As he stepped into the vestibule, he stumbled over Koroku's *geta*. Just as he was bending over to straighten them out, Koroku himself appeared. From the kitchen came Oyone's voice.

'Who is it? Sosuke?'

Sosuke greeted his brother and stepped up into the parlour. Since posting the letter he had not given Koroku a second thought. Now seeing him standing there, he felt guilty and embarrassed.

'Oyone, Oyone,' he called to his wife in the kitchen. 'Since Koroku's here, fix up something special for dinner.' Oyone hurried out of the kitchen, leaving the door open, and stood at the entrance to the parlour.

'Yes, in a minute.' She started to go back to the kitchen, but stopped.

'Koroku, would you mind putting the *amado* in place and lighting the kerosene lamp? Kiyo and I are busy in the kitchen.'

'Yes.' Koroku set himself immediately to the task.

From the kitchen came the sound of Kiyo's knife cutting vegetables and of water running. Kiyo was heard asking Oyone, 'Where shall I put this?' Then it was Koroku's

17

voice: 'Where can I find scissors to cut the wick of this lamp?' This was followed by the sound of water boiling over and sizzling on hot coals.

Sosuke sat in silence in the middle of the parlour, warming his hands over the brazier. The only colour to relieve the darkness was a tongue of red flame rising above the ashes. At that moment a daughter of the man who owned the house on the top of the cliff began to play the piano. Sosuke, called out of his reverie, rose and went onto the veranda to put the *amado* of the parlour in place. Above the bamboo trees, grey shadows against the sky, shone a star or two. The sound of the piano came from behind the bamboo thicket.

III

When Sosuke and Koroku, carrying their towels, returned from the bath, Oyone's dinner was daintily laid out on the square table in the middle of the parlour. The coals in the brazier were a more fiery red than when they had left, and the lamp was burning bright. Sosuke pulled the cushion from in front of his desk to the table and settled himself comfortably on it, cross-legged. Oyone took the soap and towel from him, asking 'How was the water?'

Sosuke gave only a grunt in reply, not a rude grunt but one that expressed relaxed contentment after the bath.

'The water was just right,' answered Koroku, turning to Oyone.

'But there were too many people,' Sosuke said languidly, drawing his knees up to the edge of the table. It was always twilight by the time he got back from work and could make his way over to the bath while Oyone prepared the evening meal. That was the hour when the place was most crowded. For the past few months he had not once seen the water transparent in the light of day. But what was worse, three or four days often passed without his getting over there at all. All week he looked forward to Sunday when he might rise early and immediately steep himself to the neck in clear hot water. But when Sunday finally came, he would prefer the leisure of a late sleep. This was, after all, the only day of the week he could indulge himself like this. As he lay languidly in bed, it seemed too much trouble to get up and go over to the bath. He would go next Sunday instead. This process repeated itself each week, almost without fail.

'It's only in the morning that I really enjoy the water,' said Sosuke.

'Then why is it that on days when you could get over there early, you spend your morning in bed?' There was a chiding tone in Oyone's voice.

Koroku secretly attributed his brother's behaviour to inborn weakness. Himself a student, he could hardly appreciate all that Sunday meant to Sosuke. Six dark, soul-stifling days and only one day of light and warmth for recovery! So much to be packed into twenty-four short hours. There was always too much that he wanted to do, and he invariably ended up spending the whole time on only one or two of the many projects he had set himself. Even as he occupied himself with these, the time would suddenly seem too valuable to be spent in this way, and while he was still worrying about the waste of precious time, the day would already draw to a close with nothing accomplished. Sosuke was so hemmed in by the circumstances of his daily life that he could find opportunity neither for the recreation of spent energies nor for the enjoyment of any hobbies. If he did not come at once to his brother's aid, it was not because he was unwilling, but rather because he lacked the mental energy for the task. This, of course, Koroku could not understand. He attributed his brother's inaction to self-centredness. He saw that Sosuke had the time for a leisurely walk about town and for quiet relaxation with his wife. And yet he did not lift a finger to help him. He was, after all, Koroku concluded, weak in brotherly affection.

Koroku had come to feel this way only quite recently — after the business with the Saekis had come up, that is. For Koroku with his youthful energy, to devise a plan was already to act upon it. When he had asked his brother to negotiate with the Saekis on his behalf, he had expected immediate action, tomorrow if not today. But when the matter had dragged along for so many weeks; when, in fact, his brother had not even made the effort to see Aunt Saeki, he was quite understandably resentful.

Still today, when after a long wait Sosuke had finally returned and he had met his brother face to face, Koroku realized that Sosuke was after all his brother, and that he spoke to him from the heart with a genuine warmth. Sosuke's brotherly attitude was disarming and he did not broach the subject of his visit at once, but accompanied him to the public bath where they had a quiet heart to heart talk.

The brothers settled themselves comfortably to their meal. Oyone did not hesitate to remain with the men at one corner of the table. Sosuke and Koroku had several cups of sake. Before beginning to eat, Sosuke, smiling, took out the *dharma* balloon he had bought on the street.

'Look at the funny balloon.' He blew it up and perched it on the edge of a bowl, pointing out its special features. Oyone and Koroku were both amused by the bloated *dharma*. Koroku blew on it. It fell from the table to the floor, but even then remained upright.

'See!' Sosuke exclaimed.

Oyone laughed aloud. She took the lid off the rice and began to serve her husband. Turning to Koroku, she said, 'Your brother still has a good bit of the child in him, hasn't he?' Her words sounded somewhat like an apology for her husband. Without a word in his own defence, Sosuke took the rice bowl from his wife and began to eat.

20

Koroku also picked up his chopsticks.

No further reference was made to the *dharma,* but it had sparked off a pleasant, unselfconscious conversation that continued throughout the meal. When they had finished eating, Koroku, in a change of mood, turned to a more serious topic.

'It's too bad about Ito,* isn't it?'

A few days before, Sosuke had read the extra carrying the news of Prince Ito's assassination and had brought the paper out to the kitchen where Oyone was working.

'Terrible news! Ito's been killed.' He had left the newspaper on top of Oyone's apron and returned to his study. Despite the content of his words, his tone of voice had been quite matter of fact.

' "Terrible news" you say, but judging from your voice, you're not particularly upset by it,' Oyone had later taken pains to remark, though half in jest. This was all that had been said of the matter. Each day's newspaper since then had carried several columns of news and commentary on the incident, but it was impossible to tell if Sosuke had read them or not, so unmoved did he seem by the whole affair. When he returned in the evening, Oyone had asked him once or twice while serving his meal,

'Did anything new come out on the Ito affair today?'

'Yes, quite a bit.' But he did not elaborate. Unless she later read for herself the newspaper she found folded in his coat pocket, she had no way of learning the day's developments. Since it served no good cause to bring up the Ito assassination in evening conversation with her husband, she made no further effort to draw him out on a topic he did not wish to discuss. Thus the affair which was causing such a stir in the outside world had been disregarded by them from the day of the extra announcing the news until Koroku had brought up the subject this evening.

---

* Ito Hirobumi (1841-1909). Select biographies of people mentioned in the text will be found at the back of the book.

'Why was he killed?' Oyone asked Koroku the same question she had put to Sosuke when she had seen the extra.

'Several bullets were pumped into him . . . a direct hit,' Koroku answered forthrightly, misunderstanding Oyone's question.

'No, *why* was he killed?' she asked again.

Koroku did not seem to have any idea as to the motive of the slaying.

'After all, it was Fate,' Sosuke asserted calmly, taking a sip of his tea, which he seemed to find to his taste. But Oyone was not satisfied with this answer.

'But why did he go to Manchuria in the first place?' she asked.

'Yes, that's the question.' Sosuke had the air of contentment after a good meal.

'They say he had some secret business with Russia,' Koroku said earnestly.

'Is that so? But it's terrible . . . to be killed like that.'

'If it had been a flunkey like me, it would be terrible, all right. But for someone like Ito, it was to his advantage to go to Harbin and be assassinated.' For the first time since the topic had come up Sosuke's voice carried expression.

'Why do you say that?' Oyone asked in surprise.

'By being assassinated he stands a good chance of becoming a famous historical figure. He could never have achieved that just by dying.'

'There's something in what you say.' Koroku seemed to accept his brother's logic, at least in part, but finally he added, 'Still, Harbin . . . in fact, all of Manchuria is a very unsettled place. I can't help feeling that there will eventually be an explosion.'

'That's because a lot of different people are converging there.'

At these words Oyone's face took on a strange expression as she looked at her husband. Sosuke seemed to take note of this, and quickly put an end to the conversation by signalling her to clear the table. He took up the *dharma* balloon again and sat it on the tip of his index finger.

'Remarkable, isn't it . . . how well it balances!'

Kiyo came out of the kitchen, took away all the dishes, then returned. Oyone followed her to make fresh tea. The two brothers were left sitting face to face.

'Ah, it's good to have the mess cleared away. I hate the sight of a table after everyone's finished eating,' Sosuke thus expressed his dislike of lingering over the dinner table once the meal was over. Frequent bursts of Kiyo's laughter could be heard in the kitchen.

'What's so funny, Kiyo?' they heard Oyone ask. Her question was greeted by another burst of laughter. The brothers sat in silence, their ears half-tuned in to Kiyo's laughter in the kitchen.

After a time Oyone returned with a tea-tray in one hand and a cake-dish in the other. From a large teapot with a wisteria-vine pattern she poured a mild, non-stimulant tea into two teacups and placed them before the men.

'What's she laughing about?' Sosuke asked. He did not look up at Oyone, but kept his eyes on the cake-dish.

'She was laughing at you . . . buying that toy and getting such a kick out of balancing it on the tip of your finger. Just like a little boy!'

'Was that all?' he said lightly. Oyone's explanation seemed to make no impression on him. But then he added, 'Even I must have been a boy at one time, I suppose.' He spoke slowly, savouring the sound of his own words. He looked up at his wife, but his eyes seemed to see beyond her. Oyone fell silent. After a long pause she broke the silence to urge Koroku to eat the cake she had placed before him, then abruptly got up and left the room. The brothers were once again alone face to face.

Since the house was far removed from the street and a full twenty-minute walk from the end of the streetcar line, the neighbourhood was even now, in early evening, extraordinarily still. Only the occasional clip-clop of *geta* could be heard outside. The night chill became more penetrating. Sosuke thrust his hands into his kimono sleeves and said,

'It's very warm during the day, but the temperature drops sharply at night, doesn't it? Do you have heat in your dormitory yet?'

'No, not yet. They never start the heating at school until it gets really cold.'

'Is that so? Then it must be very cold in your room.'

'It certainly is. But cold I can put up with. However . . .' Koroku hesitated a little, then plunged boldly ahead.

'Sosuke, what about Aunt Saeki? Oyone tells me that you sent her a letter today.'

'Yes, I did. There ought to be an answer in a couple of days. After I hear from her, I'll decide what to do next . . . whether to go to see her or not.'

Koroku silently deprecated his brother's casualness. But he saw that there was nothing in Sosuke's attitude to give offence and that he made no attempt to excuse himself for his inaction until now. Besides, after being treated to a fine meal, it was all the more difficult to come out strongly. So he merely said,

'Then you did nothing until today?' He spoke as if he wished only to ascertain the fact.

'I'm sorry, but that's true. I did nothing. Only today did I finally get round to writing a letter. But it couldn't be helped. My nerves have been bad.' He spoke with great seriousness.

Koroku smiled a wry smile. 'If the Saekis are unable to help, I'm thinking of leaving school and going off immediately to Manchuria perhaps, or Korea.'

'Manchuria? Korea? That would be quite a break with everything. But weren't you saying just a few minutes ago that Manchuria was a terrible place, a dangerously unsettled country?'

The conversation went off at a tangent. Koroku had no

24

further chance to press his point. At the end Sosuke said,
'All right. Don't worry. It'll turn out. At any rate, I'll
let you know as soon as I get an answer. We can talk the
matter over again then.' With this, the discussion ended.

As he was leaving, Koroku stepped into the next room
to say goodbye to Oyone. She was sitting before the brazier,
not doing anything.

'Goodbye, I'm leaving.'

Returning his greeting, Oyone finally rose and joined the
two brothers.

IV

Several days later, as Sosuke had expected, the answer,
which was of such importance to Koroku, came from his
aunt. But it was only a brief note. Though a postcard would
have been adequate for its contents, the sender had been
polite enough to write a short letter, enclose it in an envelope, and paste on it a three sen stamp. The handwriting was
his aunt's.

Sosuke had returned from work, changed from his close-
fitting office clothes into something more comfortable, and
was sitting before the brazier when he saw the envelope
protruding slightly from a drawer of the desk, placed there
apparently to catch his eye. He drank the tea Oyone had
set before him in a gulp and quickly broke the seal.

'What's this? Yasu's away in Kobe, it says here.'

'When did he go?' asked Oyone, who had remained at
the table after placing the teacup before her husband.

'She doesn't say. All she says is that he will return "in
the not too distant future".'

' "In the not too distant future" . . . that's certainly your
aunt's way of talking, isn't it?'

Sosuke expressed neither agreement nor disagreement
with Oyone's criticism. He folded the letter and tossed it

aside, nervously stroking his chin, which was stubbly with a four- or five-day growth of beard.

Oyone picked up the letter but made no move to read it. She rested it on her knees and looked at her husband.

' "He will return to Tokyo in the not too distant future." But is that all there is to the note? What does she mean by it?'

'What she means is that when Yasunosuke returns, she will consult him and be in touch with us again.'

' "In the not too distant future" . . . that's certainly vague enough. She doesn't really say when he'll be back.'

'That's all right.'

To make certain for herself, Oyone unfolded the letter and read it, then folded it again.

'Will you please hand me the envelope?' She stretched out her hand to her husband. Sosuke picked up the blue envelope, which lay between him and the brazier, and handed it to her. She blew into it, inserted the letter, then returned to the kitchen.

Sosuke gave no further thought to the matter. At work today, he recalled, one of the men in the office had told of meeting the English general, Kitchener, who was on a visit to Japan, near Shimbashi. A man like that, Sosuke thought, can go anywhere in the world and cause a great stir. Such a man must have been born to fame. When he compared his own fate — as it had dragged him along from the past and as it now stretched before him in the equally monotonous future — to the destiny of a man like Kitchener, the disparity between them seemed to deny that he and Kitchener shared a common humanity.

Occupied with these thoughts, Sosuke puffed away at his cigarette. Since early evening a wind had been blowing from the front of the house. It sounded to Sosuke as if it had come from a long distance determined to unleash its fury here. Occasionally it would rest and everything would be deathly still. But the stillness was filled with a greater

26

melancholy than the wind's rage. Sitting with folded arms, Sosuke thought it must be just about the time for the fire-prevention man to make his nightly round, ringing his bell and warning against fires.

He went into the kitchen and found his wife cooking slices of fish over glowing charcoal. Kiyo was at the sink washing some vegetables. Each worked busily at her task in complete silence. Sosuke stood in the doorway listening for a time to the sound of fat dripping from the fish on to the hot embers. Then without a word he closed the door and returned to his former position in front of the brazier. His wife had not lifted her eyes from the fish.

When they had finished their dinner and were sitting face to face across the brazier, Oyone once again brought up the subject of their aunt.

'They must have their problems too,' she said.

'There's nothing to be done but to wait until Yasu gets back from Kobe. It can't be helped.'

'Wouldn't it be good for you to go over and have a talk with her even before Yasu returns?'

'Possibly. But I'm sure we'll hear from her again shortly. Until then let's just wait.'

'Koroku is angry, very angry.' Oyone purposefully emphasized the point, a slight smile on her lips. Sosuke stuck the toothpick he held in his hand into the collar of his kimono.

Two days later Sosuke finally sent word to Koroku of their aunt's reply. At the end of his letter he once again assured him that everything would work out. With this, Sosuke felt rid of the burden, at least for the time being. Until the natural turn of events should force him to take it up again, it seemed simpler to forget about everything. It was in this frame of mind that he left each morning for the office and returned again each evening to his house. He was always late in getting home, and he could seldom summon the energy to go out again once he had returned. He rarely had any callers. On days when there was no special work to be done, Kiyo was even allowed to go to bed before ten o'clock. After the evening meal husband and wife would sit facing each other across the brazier and converse for about an hour. The subject of their conversation was limited to the circumstances and events of their daily life. All the same, the day to day problems of budgeting and making ends meet never came up between them. Neither ever asked, for example, how they were going to pay the grocery bill at the end of the month. It goes without saying that they never discussed literature. Moreover, they hardly ever engaged in the light and airy exchanges that characterize the conversation of a young married couple. Though they were in fact still young, they had slipped past this stage and seemed to grow plainer and more matter-of-fact day by day. To the casual observer they may even have given the impression of being two very humdrum and colourless people who had come together as man and wife only to conform to social custom. They may have given the impression too of being a very easy-going couple, an impression that would have been fortified by the seeming nonchalance with which they went about helping Koroku when he enlisted their aid.

Oyone, being a woman, was somewhat less easy-going than her husband, and once or twice tried to prod him into action. 'I wonder if Yasu has returned yet. Maybe you ought to go and have a look next Sunday.'

Sosuke answered only, 'Yes, I suppose I should.' But when the Sunday came, he seemed to have forgotten about it, and Oyone, seeing this, did not press him further. If the weather were fine, she would urge him to go out for a walk. If it were raining or windy, she would only remark that it was a good thing the day was a Sunday.

Fortunately Koroku did not come again. He was a youth of great spirit and when he set himself an aim, he would go to great lengths to achieve it. Sosuke in his student days had been like this. On the other hand, half-way towards

28

achieving his object he was quite likely to have a complete change of heart and seem to forget what had gone before, carrying on as if the project he had been working so hard to accomplish were really of no consequence after all. In this too the brothers were alike. Sosuke also had once been like this. Moreover, Koroku had a relatively good head. Whether it was that his emotions generally followed the direction of his reason or that his reason jumped in to justify his emotions, he could not be satisfied unless a course of action were reasonable. And once its reasonableness became apparent, he set himself upon it with great passion as something to be achieved. Since he was of a strong constitution and possessed great energy, he was able to place reliance upon his youthful vitality in whatever he did.

Every time he looked at his brother, Sosuke couldn't help feeling as if he were looking at his old self, alive again and active before his eyes. At times this made him fearful and occasionally it caused him bitter pain. Then it seemed to him that heaven was purposely parading Koroku before him to recall to mind as often as possible the bitter memory of the simple, sincere youth he himself had once been, and he shuddered at the thought. When he reflected that his brother might have been born to the same fate as himself, he became all the more troubled, and even despondent.

Until now, Sosuke had never expressed opinions to his brother or given him anything approaching advice for the future. He treated him in a most commonplace and ordinary manner. Just as his present way of life was so sober as to belie the fact that he was a man with a past, so in treatment of his brother there was almost nothing in his manner to suggest that he was older and had ever had anything worthy of the name of experience.

Since there had been two other brothers, who had died young, between Sosuke and Koroku, there was a ten-year difference in their ages. Moreover, in his first year of university Sosuke had for various reasons transferred to Kyoto, so that he had lived in the same house with his brother only until the latter was twelve or thirteen. Sosuke could remember Koroku as he had been at that time, a headstrong, mischievous boy. Their father was then still alive, and the family was relatively well-off. They lived comfortably and could even afford to employ their own *jinrikisha* man and to provide a house for him in the grounds. This *jinrikisha* driver had a boy about three years younger than Koroku, and the two always played together. One very hot summer's day the two boys had tied a bag of candy to the end of a pole and were standing at the foot of a large persimmon tree trying to catch cicadas. Seeing them, Sosuke called out to the other boy, 'Kenbo, if you stand bareheaded too long under the open sun, you'll get sunstroke,' and he handed him Koroku's old straw hat. When he saw his brother give away something that belonged to him without his permission, Koroku became angry. He quickly snatched the hat from the boy's hands, threw it to the ground, and stamped on it, crushing it completely. Sosuke jumped down from the veranda in his bare feet and struck Koroku a blow on the head. From that time on Sosuke recognized a strain of meanness in his brother.

In his second year Sosuke had had to leave the university, in circumstances which made it impossible for him to return home. From Kyoto he went directly to Hiroshima, and after spending half a year in that city his father died. His mother had preceded him six years earlier. There now remained only Koroku, who was sixteen, and the twenty-five-year-old mistress his father had taken after his wife's death.

Upon receiving a telegram from the Saekis informing him of his father's death, Sosuke had come to Tokyo, for the first time in many months. When the funeral was over, he began to look into his father's affairs as a prelude to settling the estate. He was surprised to find that the property, which he had thought to be quite considerable, was in reality very little, and that his father's debts, which he had thought to be non-existent, amounted to quite a large sum. When he consulted his Uncle Saeki, the latter advised him to sell the house. He decided to give his father's mistress a large sum of money and send her off at once, and he arranged for Koroku to live with his uncle for the present. It was impossible, however, to find a buyer for the house at such short notice, and so Sosuke, since there was no other way, asked his uncle to raise the money needed and settle the debts.

Saeki was a businessman who was always trying his hand at money-making ventures that inevitably failed. He was something of a speculator. While Sosuke was still living at home, Saeki had time after time, with great eloquence, persuaded his father to invest in his crackpot schemes. And since his father too, it seemed, had a thirst for easy profits, he poured a considerable amount of money into Saeki's 'good bargains'.

Even at the time of his father's death, Saeki did not seem to be making out any better than usual, but since he felt himself under some obligation to Sosuke's father and since he knew from experience that no matter how hard pressed he might be, something always turned up when it was most needed, he readily agreed to pay off the debts and settle the estate. In return, Sosuke left the sale of the house entirely to his discretion. What it amounted to, then, was that in return for raising money in a hurry to take care of the debts, the house and the land on which it stood were, in effect, given to Saeki. 'After all, I stand to take a great loss, if I can't find a buyer,' explained the uncle.

The bulk of the furnishings and equipment of the house, which was not of much value, was sold off. In the case of five or six *kakemono* and a number of antique pieces, Saeki thought it would be a loss not to search patiently for a buyer eager to have them. Sosuke agreed with him and entrusted these also to his care. There still remained in ready cash about two thousand yen, but Sosuke realized that part of this money would have to be used to pay for Koroku's education. He was reluctant to take the money himself and make a commitment to send a monthly allowance to his brother, since his present position was extremely unstable, and such a commitment might later prove very difficult to carry out. It was a hard decision to make, but he resolutely turned half of the sum over to his uncle for Koroku. He had made a mess of his own life, but he wanted Koroku at least to make a success of his. Sosuke also extended to his brother the vague promise that when the thousand yen had been spent he would try to find some way of making further provision. Then he returned to Hiroshima.

Just half a year later a letter in his uncle's handwriting came to him saying that the house had finally been sold and that he could set his mind at ease on the matter. It did not say for how much it was sold, and when Sosuke wrote back to inquire, two weeks passed before he received the vague answer that he shouldn't worry, since the amount had been fully adequate to compensate for the expenses which he — Saeki — had incurred in settling the estate. Sosuke, of course, felt no little dissatisfaction with this reply also. Since Saeki promised to give him the details when they met, he thought of going to Tokyo at once. But when he broached the matter to Oyone, she looked at him with a sad smile and said simply,

'But it's impossible for you to go there *now*. There's nothing to be done about it.'

At these words he felt like a man who has for the first time received a verdict from his wife. He sat for a while with folded arms and reflected. He saw that Oyone was right: he was so chained by his circumstances that plan as he might he could not get away, and he gave up the idea.

Since he could not go to Tokyo, he exchanged three or four more letters with Saeki, but the answer was always the same. It could have been rubber-stamped, 'I will give you all the details when I see you.'

'All right, then! I've got to go to Tokyo.' With angry face, Sosuke looked at Oyone.

Three months later an opportunity to get away finally presented itself and he prepared to take Oyone with him, their first visit to Tokyo for a long time. But on the eve of their departure he came down with a bad cold that developed into typhoid fever, and he had to remain in bed for more than sixty days. For thirty days after that he was still too weak even to do his work as he should.

Shortly after recovering from his illness, it became necessary for him to transfer from Hiroshima to Fukuoka. Just before making the move, he thought he saw another chance of getting to Tokyo, but this time also a number of things came up to prevent him from going. Finally he entrusted his fate to the southbound train taking him ever farther away from Tokyo. By this time the money he had received at the time of his father's death was almost exhausted. The two years or so in Fukuoka were spent in a hard struggle. He often recalled his student days in Kyoto when under all kinds of pretexts he had solicited and obtained from his father large sums of money to use as he wished. He compared his present state to that of his Kyoto days. He was struck by the inexorability of his fate and he shuddered. At times, thinking back over the springtime of his youth, which had passed by so imperceptibly, he realized that those days had been the high point of his life, and with eyes newly awakened to that realization, he looked back upon them to what seemed the distant and misty past. Finally, the situation became almost more than he could bear and he said to Oyone,

'I've let things drift for a long time, but now I'm thinking again of going to Tokyo.'

Oyone, of course, did not oppose him. She merely looked down and said, 'It's no use thinking about it. Still, I have absolutely no trust in your uncle.' Her voice was cheerless.

'I suppose from his point of view, we're the ones that aren't to be trusted, but it's certainly true that we have no trust in him.' Sosuke spoke with vivacity, but when he saw Oyone's disheartened look, his courage quickly drained away.

This kind of exchange occurred between them about once or twice a month at first, then only once every two months, and later still, about once every third month. Finally he told Oyone,

'If only Koroku is being properly taken care of! As for the rest, it can wait until I go to Tokyo and have a talk with my uncle. There's nothing else to be done, is there, Oyone?'

'That should be all right,' she agreed.

Sosuke let the matter drop. In the face of what had happened in the past, he did not feel as if he could make representations to his uncle on his own behalf, and in fact he had never done so in any of his letters up to the present time. He received an occasional note from Koroku, usually very brief and formal. Sosuke still had in mind the Koroku he had met in Tokyo at the time of his father's death, and thought of him as little more than a boy. Thus it never occurred to him, of course, to ask Koroku to act as his representative in negotiations with their uncle.

The couple lived in retirement from the world. When the cold was hard to bear, they found warmth in each other's embrace, relying only on one another. When the pain was most acute, Oyone would always say to Sosuke,

'But it can't be helped.'

And Sosuke would answer, 'We'll bear up under it!'

They shared at all times a kind of stoic forbearance or resignation to fate. Almost no ray of hope for the future ever reached them. They spoke little of the past, and at times it even seemed as if they had mutually agreed to avoid the subject. Occasionally Oyone would try to console her husband.

34

'Something good is sure to happen. This chain of bad luck is bound to break.'

When she spoke in this way, Sosuke felt as if the poisoned tongue of Fate were making use of his wife's heartfelt words to taunt him. He would say nothing, but only smile bitterly. Oyone, still unaware of his feelings, would continue resolutely:

'We have the right to look forward to better times.'

But finally she would notice the effect of her words on her husband, and seal her lips, And so, as the two sat facing each other in silence, they would suddenly find themselves at the bottom of the deep dark pit of the past which they themselves had dug.

The stain of their sin had besmeared their future. They were resigned to the fact that no colourful vistas lay ahead of them in the path they walked, and they were content to stumble along, hand in hand. From the beginning Sosuke had not placed much expectation in the property his uncle had sold for them. But occasionally he would speak of it in the following fashion:

'With the present state of the market, even if my uncle sold the property for almost nothing, the money he got for it would still be at least twice the amount he raised to pay off the debt.'

Oyone would smile sadly, and remonstrate, 'The property again! Don't you ever think of anything else? Aren't you the one who entrusted the whole matter to your uncle?'

'It couldn't be helped. There was no other way at the time.'

'He probably got the impression that you were giving him the house and the land in return for the money he spent in clearing the debts.'

Oyone's words made Sosuke realize that there might be something to be said after all in defence of his uncle's management of the estate. But aloud he said,

'That was a mistaken impression.' Still the matter gradually faded farther and farther into the background.

One day after the couple had been living for two years in this lonely but intimate fashion, Sosuke chanced to meet a former classmate, who had been a good friend of his during his student days, a man named Sugihara. After graduation Sugihara had passed the higher civil service examination and was now employed in a government ministry. He had come to Fukuoka and Saga on ministry business. Sosuke had learned from the newspaper when he would arrive and where he would stay, but he had no intention of visiting him at his hotel. It would be too humiliating for a loser like himself to have to bow his head before a success like Sugihara, and so he wished above all to avoid a meeting with this old friend of university days.

But Sugihara, through some chance connection, had heard that Sosuke was wasting his talents in an obscure job in Fukuoka, and he made a point of looking him up. When he saw that the meeting could not be avoided, Sosuke swallowed his pride and met Sugihara. It was through Sugihara that Sosuke was finally able to move back to Tokyo. When he received a letter from Sugihara saying that everything had been arranged, Sosuke put down his chopsticks and said,

'Oyone, we're finally on our way to Tokyo!'

'That's fine, I supopse.' She looked into her husband's face as she spoke.

The first two or three weeks after their arrival in Tokyo sped by fast enough to make their heads spin. There was the hectic business of setting up a new household and beginning a new job. There was also the excitement of breathing once again the air of the big city with its vibrant energy that never let up day or night. They found no time to sit down and think leisurely about anything, and they lacked the good sense to make themselves do so.

When they arrived by train at Shimbashi, they saw the

Saekis for the first time in several years. It may have been the lights on the platform, but to Sosuke's eye neither his aunt nor his uncle seemed to be in good spirits. There had been an accident along the way and the train had arrived thirty minutes behind schedule — an unusual occurrence. The Saekis looked as if they were tired of waiting and had fixed the blame for the delay on Sosuke.

'Sosuke, how you've aged since we saw you last,' had been his aunt's only greeting. Sosuke then introduced his wife, whom they had never met.

'Is she the one. . . . ?' His aunt hesitated and looked at Sosuke. Oyone was at a loss to know what to say and remained silent, head bowed.

Koroku, of course, had also come along to meet them. When Sosuke first caught sight of his younger brother, he was surprised to see how he had grown, even to the point of overtaking him. Koroku had just finished middle school and was about to enter high school. Seeing Sosuke, he neither addressed him as brother, nor welcomed him back to Tokyo. He merely mumbled a few clumsy words.

Sosuke and Oyone stayed for a week in a hotel and then moved into their present home. During this period, the Saekis had been a great help. They had insisted that if Oyone were satisfied with second-hand things, there was no need to buy such items as kitchen utensils and the like, as they would provide them; and they did in fact send them the dishes and utensils for several settings. They even gave them sixty yen, saying,

'Since you're getting started anew, there must be many things you have to buy.'

While they were thus distracted with the many details of getting settled in Tokyo, half a year passed. The problem which had weighed so heavily on their minds when they were living in Hiroshima and Fukuoka, that of the family property, had still not been touched in conversation with the Saekis. Oyone one day asked her husband if he had discussed the matter with his uncle yet.

'No, not yet,' he replied. He sounded as if he had forgotten about it until she had reminded him.

'That's strange . . . when you had it so much on your mind before,' she said, smiling.

'But I haven't had the time yet to discuss the matter calmly,' said Sosuke in his own defence.

Ten more days passed. This time it was Sosuke who said to his wife, 'Oyone, I still haven't said anything. Somehow or other, I hate to bring up the subject.'

'Then don't bring it up.'

'Is it all right if I don't?'

'Why do you ask me? It's your concern. Do as you like.'

'It seems a bit strange to bring the matter up formally at this time. If I have a chance to put the question to him casually, I'll do so. I ought to be able to find an opening before too long.' And so he put the matter off still longer.

Koroku received adequate care at his uncle's home. He seemed to have already consulted his uncle about entering a school dormitory, should he succeed in passing the high school entrance examination. Perhaps because his brother, who had only now moved to Tokyo, had never concerned himself personally with his school expenses, Koroku did not confide in him as intimately as he did in his uncle. He was also on very good terms with his cousin, Yasunosuke. In fact, Yasunosuke seemed to him more like his own brother than Sosuke.

Sosuke's visits to his uncle naturally became less and less frequent, and since even these occasional visits were mostly a matter of form, he always felt keenly dissatisfied when he was on his way home. The visits became more and more distasteful to him, and finally no sooner would he arrive and exchange greetings with his uncle and aunt than he would already think of taking his leave. He found it difficult to keep up a general conversation with his uncle, even during the half hour or so he sat and talked with him. His uncle too seemed somewhat uncomfortable. His aunt would try to detain him with such words as 'I'm sure you can stay for a while longer,' but this would only make him the more eager to leave at once. Yet if he stayed away for too long a time, he would feel ill at ease, as if he had done something wrong, and he would go to see them again. Sometimes he would even bow his head and thank them for the care they were taking of Koroku. But he could never bring himself to speak of his brother's future school expenses or of the disposition his uncle had made of the family property. Still, it was not simply out of a sense of duty towards a blood relative or out of the desire to keep up appearances before the world that he continued to visit his uncle. It was clear that deep within him lay the desire to settle this matter of the house, should an opportunity to do so present itself.

'Sosuke's changed completely,' the aunt had remarked one day to her husband.

'So he has. But after all, that business was bound to have repercussions for a long time afterwards,' answered the uncle, reflecting upon the fearful law of retribution that attends a man's misdeeds.

'It's really frightening, isn't it?' his wife continued. 'He always used to be so full of life . . . in fact, too full of life, the way he would carry on! He wasn't an old stick as he is now. In the two or three years he has been away, he's grown so old. He looks even older than you.'

'Hardly!'

'No, I mean it. Maybe not his head or face, but the overall impression he makes,' his wife pursued her point.

This conversation between uncle and aunt had taken place more than once since Sosuke had come to Tokyo. The fact was that whenever he visited the Saekis Sosuke did appear as his aunt described him.

Oyone, for reasons of her own, met the Saekis only that once at Shimbashi Station, when she was introduced to them by her husband. After that she never once crossed the threshold of their home. She always spoke politely of them as 'aunt' and 'uncle', but when Sosuke would invite her to accompany him on one of his visits, she would thank him and bow her head, but in the end would not go. Finally even Sosuke, for all his casualness, urged her more strongly.

'How about going with me at least this once?'

'But. . . .' She hesitated and made a strange face. Seeing her reluctance, Sosuke said no more and he never again repeated the invitation.

The two families continued in this way for about a year. Then suddenly the uncle, whom the aunt had thought to be younger in spirit than Sosuke, died. The cause of his death was diagnosed as spinal meningitis. He had been in bed for two or three days with what was thought to be just a cold. While he was washing his hands on the way back from the toilet, he collapsed, the water dipper still in his hands. In less than a day he was dead.

'Oyone, uncle died finally without my ever speaking to him,' said Sosuke.

'Were you still intending to ask him about that? You never give up, do you?' answered Oyone.

Another year passed. Saeki's son, Yasunosuke, graduated from university and Koroku became a second-year high school student. Saeki's wife moved with Yasunosuke to another part of Tokyo, Naka roku bancho.

In the summer of his third year at high school, Koroku went to Boshu, a fine place for swimming on the eastern seacoast. He stayed there over a month. It was already early September when he left Boshu, cut across from Hota to the Kazusa sea-shore, and followed along the coast to Choshi. Then, realizing it was time to get back, he returned to Tokyo. No more than two or three days after his return, on an afternoon still hot with the lingering heat of summer, he suddenly arrived at Sosuke's. His face was darkly tanned, bringing out the whiteness of his eyes and giving him an unfamiliar, wild appearance. Though it had been a long time since his last visit, he made himself at home immediately, stretching himself out on the *tatami* to await his brother's return. As soon as he caught sight of Sosuke coming through the gate, he rose quickly to greet him as he entered.

'There's something I want to see you about.'

Sosuke was surprised at the urgency in his voice and heard him out at once, not even taking the time to change from his office clothes into a *yukata*.

Koroku's story was this. The evening of his return from Kazusa his aunt had told him that she was sorry but that after New Year's Day she would no longer be able to pay his school fees. Koroku was stunned. Ever since he had gone to live with his uncle immediately after his father's death, he had never had to worry about anything. He had been able to go to school, he had had his clothes taken care of for him, and he had even received an adequate allowance for personal expenses. There was nothing that he lacked, just as it had been when his father was still alive. He had taken everything for granted, so that until that day, that evening, he had never even given a thought to school fees. He was so completely taken aback by his aunt's declaration that he just stood there, at a loss for words.

Woman that she was, his aunt had spent about an hour in a long, involved explanation of why she could no longer provide for him and of how sorry she was about it. There was her husband's death, and the resulting change in their financial status, and Yasunosuke's graduation from college, and now the problem of his marriage — all these elements entered into it.

'If possible, I wanted to continue to help you, at least until you graduated from high school, and so I have made many sacrifices up to now.'

It was then that Koroku remembered that when Sosuke had come to Tokyo for their father's funeral and was about to return to Hiroshima after making the necessary arrangements, he had told him that money for his education had been deposited with his uncle. He mentioned this to his aunt, but she made a strange face and said,

'It's true that Sosuke did give your uncle a certain amount of money for your education, but it's all gone. In fact, even while your uncle was still alive, he was paying your school expenses at the end.'

Since his brother had never told him the amount of the money that had been deposited or for how many years of schooling the calculation had been made, there was nothing he could say.

'But you aren't alone. You have a brother. Why don't you talk it over with him? I'll also go to see him and explain everything. He hasn't come over for a long time and I haven't been to see him either. So I've had no chance to take the matter up with him,' his aunt had added at the end of the conversation.

When Koroku had finished, Sosuke looked into his face and said only, 'This is a big problem!' He did not get angry and immediately run over to his aunt's house to confront her, as he would have done in the old days. Nor, on the other hand, did he seem to take offence at the change of attitude in his brother, who until now had treated him almost as a stranger, inasmuch as he had not to rely on him in any way.

It was a very disturbed Koroku that Sosuke saw to the door that evening, a Koroku who seemed to be blaming others for the fact that the brilliant future he had visualized now lay half in shambles. Sosuke watched his brother's retreating figure until it was out of sight and then continued to stand for a time in the darkened doorway, looking at the last rays of the setting sun.

That evening Sosuke cut two large leaves from the Basho trees at the back, spread them out on the veranda floor, and he and Oyone sat there in the evening cool discussing Koroku.

'I wonder if your aunt is thinking that we should provide for Koroku,' Oyone remarked.

'We can't know what she's thinking until we see her and find out.'

'I'm sure that must be it,' insisted Oyone, as she fanned herself. The veranda was now quite dark. Sosuke did not answer her, but looked up at the colour of the narrow strip of sky between the cliff and the eaves of the house. The two remained silent for a time. Then Oyone spoke again.

'But we can't do it.'

'It's beyond my power to put a boy through college.' Sosuke made clear that he was not up to such a feat.

The conversation then turned to another subject and did not come back to Koroku or their aunt.

Two days later happened to be a Saturday, and so on his way home from the office Sosuke called on his aunt.

'My! What a rare treat!' exclaimed his aunt, receiving him with a greater display of affection than usual. This time Sosuke plunged at once into the unpleasant business of asking for the first time the questions that had been accumulating for four or five years. His aunt, of course, defended herself and her husband as best she could.

She did not remember exactly how much her husband had received for the sale of Sosuke's father's house and property, but when he had deducted from it the money he had used to pay off the debts, 4,500 yen were left, or was it 4,300? Her husband was under the impression that Sosuke had really given him the house and that whatever money he made from the sale might be looked upon as his own. Still, since he didn't want it to be said that he had made a profit from the sale of Sosuke's house, he decided to deposit the money in Koroku's name, making it Koroku's property. He thought that since Sosuke had done what he did, he

43

deserved to be disinherited. He had no longer the right to even a sen.

'Sosuke, don't get angry. I'm only repeating what your uncle said,' his aunt interjected. Sosuke listened in silence to the rest of what she had to tell him.

The money which was to have been deposited in Koroku's name was, unfortunately, invested by his uncle in a shop on a busy street in Kanda. But before it was even possible to get insurance coverage, the place burned down. Since Koroku had been told nothing of the arrangement, they purposely left him in ignorance of it.

'I'm sorry for you too, Sosuke, but it couldn't be helped. There was nothing that could be done about it. It was just a case of bad luck. Of course, if your uncle had lived, he would have made it up to him in some way. One person more would not have posed so much of a problem. And even now with your uncle gone, if it were possible I would give Koroku a sum of money equivalent to the value of the house that burned down, or at least provide for him somehow until he graduated from the university.' Then his aunt turned to her own problem of Yasunosuke's employment.

Yasunosuke, her only son, had graduated from college only that summer. Inasmuch as he had led a very sheltered life at home and had had fewer social contacts than other young men of his age, he had little knowledge of the world. After graduation he was going out into the world, of which he knew so little, armed only with technical learning. His subject was applied mechanical engineering and even today when enthusiasm for business enterprise was at a low ebb, there were certainly a few companies of the many in Japan that could make use of his technical knowledge.

But he too, it seemed, had something of the speculator in him, inherited from his father. He wanted to try to make it on his own. He happened to meet a graduate of the same engineering department as himself, a few years older than he, who had built his own little factory at Tsukishima and

44

was operating it himself. After talking things over with this fellow graduate, he decided that he wanted to invest some capital in this enterprise and join in the venture. This was the family problem.

'We sold the few stocks we had and invested our money in that factory, so that we are now, in effect, almost penniless. I suppose that in the eyes of the world at large we seem to be quite well-off, since there are just the two of us living in this fine house. The other day when Hara's mother called, she remarked that there was no one better off than we were, that whenever she visited us she could not help envying our life of leisurely contentment. But the facts are quite different.'

After hearing his aunt's explanation, Sosuke could only stand there. No words came to his lips. This, he knew, was the result of his nervous condition. He took it as further proof that he no longer had the wit to come to a quick judgment, that was both clear and penetrating, as he once had had. His aunt, thinking it must be impossible for Sosuke to accept the truth of her words, even specified the amount of money Yasunosuke had invested. (It was 5,000 yen.) For the time being, they had to live on Yasunosuke's low salary and the income from the stocks.

'And we're not even sure about the returns yet. If all goes well, we will receive ten to fifteen per cent dividend, but one mistake and it could all very well go up in smoke,' his aunt added.

Sosuke was inwardly troubled. Nothing his aunt had done appeared to him particularly reprehensible, but he felt it would be very unwise to leave without coming to some understanding with regard to Koroku's future. He had nothing more to say about the present problem, but he inquired instead about the disposition of the thousand yen entrusted to his uncle for Koroku's education.

'Sosuke, please believe me. That has been used entirely

for Koroku. Since entering high school even, some 700 yen have been spent,' she answered.

Sosuke turned to another point and asked as casually as possible what had happened to the *kakemono* and antiques left with his uncle for disposal.

'Oh, those! That was really foolish!' she exclaimed. Then, seeing the look on Sosuke's face, she asked,

'You mean you've never heard about it?'

Sosuke shook his head, and she continued.

'What a shame! Your uncle must have forgotten to tell you,' and she proceeded to give him the details.

Soon after Sosuke had returned to Hiroshima, his uncle had asked an acquaintance of his by the name of Sanada to look after the sale of the articles. He was supposed to be a man experienced in such matters, who spent a great deal of time frequenting art and antique dealers. The man immediately agreed to undertake the sale, but what followed was this. He would come to Saeki saying, 'I've found a buyer for such and such an antique, so please may I have it to show to him?'; or else, 'Mr So-and-So is interested in such and such a *kakemono* and wants to see it.' In this way he got all the articles into his possession, and they never came back. When questioned, he would proffer a number of excuses, such as that the prospective buyer was still looking at it. They could never get a satisfactory answer from him, and finally he seems to have gone out of business and disappeared completely.

'But there is still one folding screen left. It turned up when we moved the other day, and Yasu said, "This screen is Sosuke's. When we have the chance, let's take it to him." '

His aunt spoke of the articles that had been left with the Saekis as if she thought them of little value. Sosuke too, who had never given them a thought until today, had never been much interested in them. For that reason he could not very well be angry with his aunt for not seeming to have the slightest conscience about their disappearance. Still, when

46

his aunt said, 'Sosuke, we have no use here for this screen, why don't you take it along with you? They say that such things bring a very nice price these days,' he suddenly felt like taking it home.

She took the screen out of the store-room for him, and when he looked at it in the light, he remembered its two folding panels. At the bottom, covering the full width of the panels, were painted grasses of all kinds: the *hagi*, the *kikyo*, the *susuki*, the *kuzu*, the *ominaeshi*. At the top in silver was a full moon and in the open space to the side of of it was written the title 'The *Ominaeshi* Flower Between the Moon and a Country Path', a phrase from a poem by Kiichi. Sosuke bent down and closely inspected the painter's signature, Hoitsu, written in a flowing scrawl, beginning at a corner of the silver moon that had been scorched black and continuing through the dry brown leaves, whose backs were turned upwards by the wind. The signature was enclosed in a large red circle the size of a *daifuku* charm. Sosuke could not help recalling the days when his father was still alive.

At the beginning of each year his father would bring this screen out of the dark store-room, stand it in the vestibule, and place before it a square, rosewood box for callers to leave their New Year's greetings. Since it was an auspicious season, he always hung a painting of a tiger in the alcove of the parlour. Sosuke remembered his father telling him, 'It's a painting by Gantai, not by Ganku.' On the tiger there was a black smudge. The tiger was lapping water with its tongue from the valley river, and on the ridge of its nose was a smear of Indian ink, which had upset his father very much. Even in later years he would ask Sosuke if he remembered having smeared Indian ink on the tiger. 'You did it when you were a little boy.' He spoke half in amusement, half in regret.

Sosuke sat solenmly in front of the screen, calling to mind scenes of his life in Tokyo so long ago.

47

'I'll take the screen with me, then,' he told his aunt.

'Yes, please do.' Then she added, 'I'll ask someone to deliver it.' There was no mistaking her good will.

Sosuke agreed to this and putting an end to the conversation returned home. That evening after dinner he and Oyone went out to the veranda again to cool themselves. As they sat together, their white *yukata* standing out against the dark of the veranda, Sosuke gave Oyone a report of the conversation with his aunt.

'You didn't meet Yasu?' Oyone asked.

'Yasu's at the factory till late every day, including Saturdays.'

'He must be working very hard.' That was all she said. She added not a single word of criticism for the irresponsible way the Saekis had mismanaged the sale of the articles.

'Poor Koroku! What will happen to him?' asked Sosuke.

'Yes, I wonder,' was all that Oyone replied.

'We have a pretty strong case but if we were to insist, we would probably end up in court, and lacking proof, we stand no chance of winning,' said Sosuke, foreseeing one possible, but extreme, line of action.

'It's better not to take it to court, even if we could win,' quickly answered Oyone. Sosuke too rejected that possibility.

'This is all because I wasn't able to come to Tokyo that time.'

'And when you were able to come, it no longer made any difference.'

Without interrupting their conversation they looked out at the narrow strip of sky visible above the eaves and, still speculating about the next day's weather, went back into the house and under the mosquito netting to prepare for bed.

The following Sunday Sosuke invited Koroku over, and he reported to him everything their aunt had said.

48

'I don't know why she didn't give you a full explanation. Perhaps it was because she knows how short-tempered you are, or else it may be because she thinks you are still a child, and she gave you a simplified account on purpose. At any rate, the facts are as I have just stated them.'

No explanation, however detailed, could assuage Koroku's anger. He said only, 'Is that so?' and stared at Sosuke with a stern, dissatisfied face.

'It couldn't be helped. Neither your aunt nor Yasu meant badly.'

'I know that,' said Koroku, sternly.

'I suppose you think that I'm to blame. . . . Of course, I am. Through the years I've been to blame for many things.'

Sosuke lay on his side on the *tatami*, smoking his cigarette. He said nothing more. Koroku too was silent. He stood looking at the two-panelled folding screen in one corner of the room.

'Do you remember that screen?' asked Sosuke, breaking the silence at last.

'Yes, I do.'

'The Saekis sent it over the day before yesterday. Of all father's things, this alone remains. If this could be of some help with your school expenses, I'd gladly give it to you right away. But you can't get through college on one old faded screen.' Sosuke laughed a bitter laugh and added, 'It must seem crazy to you to put this screen up now in this hot weather, but there's no place to store it. It can't be helped.'

Koroku always felt dissatisfied with his brother, so easygoing and nonchalant, so different and so distant from himself. Still, when it came right down to it, he could never really pick a quarrel with him. Now also the force of his anger diminished and he said only,

'Do what you want with the screen. But what about me? What am I to do now?'

'That's the problem. At any rate, we have to the end of

49

the year to decide. Think about it carefully, and I will too.'

By nature Koroku found such a temporizing attitude repellent. He pleaded earnestly with his brother. When he went to class, he lacked the peace of mind to concentrate. He could no longer even prepare his lessons. This was all more than he could bear. Sosuke listened to him, but his attitude remained unchanged. When Koroku's litany of complaints reached too shrill a peak, he said calmly.

'If you feel so dissatisfied, why don't you do something else? There no reason why you shouldn't leave school. You're certainly far fitter than I am.'

Koroku saw that it was no use prolonging the conversation and he returned to his lodging in Hongo.

After his brother had gone, Sosuke took a hot bath and had dinner. After dinner he and Oyone went for a walk among the street stalls that had been set up for the local shrine festival. At one of these stalls they bought two potted plants and each carried one home. Thinking it better for the plants to be exposed to the night dew, Sosuke opened one of the windows on the cliff side and placed the plants side by side on the window ledge. When they had stepped under the mosquito netting and were preparing for bed, Oyone asked her husband,

'What's to be done about Koroku?'

'I don't know yet,' Sosuke answered. Ten minutes later husband and wife were sound asleep.

When he awoke the next morning, Sosuke took up again the routine of a week of work, and he had no time to give further thought to Koroku. Even at the end of the day's work, when he could enjoy a bit of leisure, he refrained from bringing the problem into clear focus and looking squarely at it. The thinking apparatus concealed within his shock of hair was not up to dealing with the complexities of the case. In the old days he had liked mathematics and had had the mental agility to chart even complicated geometry problems clearly in his head. When he recalled the

50

past, the change that had come over him with such fury in so short a time was enough to frighten him.

About once a day the image of Koroku would come vaguely to the surface of his mind and for a moment he would have the feeling that he had to do some serious thinking about his brother's future. But this was quickly superceded by the idea that there was no need to hurry, one thought cancelling out the other. And so he lived out each day as if his emotions were stultifying.

September was drawing to a close. Every night a great host of stars was visible in the Milky Way. On one of these nights Yasunosuke dropped in for a visit. He might as well have fallen from the sky. He was so rare a visitor that both Sosuke and Oyone were very surprised to see him and guessed at once that he had come on business. As he had. He had come to discuss Koroku.

A few days earlier Koroku had suddenly turned up at the factory in Tsukishima. His brother, he said, had given him a detailed explanation concerning the matter of his school fees. Until the present he had lived the life of a student and he would be very sorry to have this life ended now, without his going on to college. He was willing to do anything, even get into debt, just as long as he was able to go as far as his talents would take him. He wanted to know if Yasu knew of any way that he might realize his ambition. Yasunosuke had answered that he would speak to Sosuke. But Koroku had broken in immediately to say that his brother was not one to consult on such a matter. Since Sosuke himself had never graduated from college, he considered it almost natural to break off studies somewhere along the way. Although Sosuke was basically responsible for what had happened to him, Koroku, he seemed to be unconcerned about him and to pay no attention to anything he said. For that reason Yasu was the only person he could rely on. Having been formally refused by his aunt, it might seem very strange for him to turn now to his cousin, but he had come anyway, thinking that Yasu would be better able to understand his position than his aunt.

Nothing Yasunosuke said could make Koroku change his mind. Yasunosuke had consoled him saying that he was wrong in thinking his brother unconcerned. In fact, Sosuke was very much worried about him and would be dropping in to discuss the matter one of these days. Before he left, Koroku asked Yasunosuke to put his seal on a number of class absentee slips, saying,

'I can't really get down to studying until I know whether I'm to leave school or to go on. As long as everything is so uncertain, there's no need to go to class every day.' Then he took his departure.

Yasunosuke left Sosuke's after less than an hour, saying that he was very busy. No concrete plan for Koroku emerged from their conversation. Yasunosuke's parting suggestion was that all concerned — including Koroku, if this were convenient — get together and decide upon a course of action. When the two were alone again, Oyone asked Sosuke,

'What do you think?'

Sosuke stuck both of his hands into his sash and raised his shoulders slightly.

'If I could only be like Koroku again! I keep fearing that he'll fall into Fate's snare as I have. On the other hand, he hardly gives any thought to me. But it's better that way!'

Oyone cleared away the tea things and carried them into the kitchen. The two spoke no further of the matter, but laid out their bedding for the night and went to sleep. High above them as they slept the stars of the Milky Way shone down coolly.

The following week Koroku did not appear, nor was there any message from their aunt. Sosuke's home returned again to its usual uneventfulness. The couple rose each morning while the dew was still sparkling on the grass, and they could look out to see a beautiful sun begin to rise

52

above the eaves of the house. Every evening they would sit on either side of the lamp in its smoked bamboo holder, casting long shadows across walls and ceiling. During the pauses in their conversation the quiet became intense and not infrequently the only sound to be heard was that of the swinging pendulum of the wall clock.

The two talked about Koroku. Whether he continued school or not, he would have to leave his present lodging. In that case there were only two places he could go. He could return to the Saekis or come to live with Sosuke. Although their aunt had spoken her mind so clearly, out of good will she would probably agree to keep Koroku at her home for the time being, if she were asked to do so. But as for Koroku's school expenses — tuition, spending money, and other incidentals — Sosuke saw that this would have to be his responsibilty. He saw too that this would be more than the house budget could bear. When they made a careful calculation of their monthly income and expenditures, they had to conclude,

'We just can't manage it.'

'It's absolutely impossible.'

Next to the parlour in which the two sat was the kitchen. To the right of the kitchen was a room for the maid and to the left was another small room. Since there were just the three of them, including the maid, Oyone had no real use for this room and kept her dressing-table there, near the window on the east side. Sosuke too, upon rising, would wash his face, have breakfast, then go there to change his clothes.

'Or else, what about giving Koroku the room next to the kitchen?' Oyone suggested. She thought that perhaps if they provided Koroku with bed and board, they might be able to get the Saekis to pay so much a month towards his other expenses. Thus Koroku could realize his cherished wish of continuing with his education until he graduated.

'As for clothes, he could probably get along with some

53

of Yasu's old things, or yours. I could make them over for him,' she added. Sosuke had also been thinking along these lines, but the idea had not taken precise form, because he hesitated to ask that much of Oyone, and so he had not put it into words. But, on the contrary, when she herself now made the proposal, he had not the courage to oppose it.

Sosuke wrote a letter to Koroku telling him of their plan. If Koroku had no objection to it, he would go once again to talk to the Saekis. The evening of the very day he received the letter, Koroku hurried over to Sosuke's, with the rain pattering down on his umbrella, as happy as if he had already received the financial help he needed.

'Your aunt spoke as she did,' suggested Oyone, 'because she saw that we weren't doing anything for you. Of course, your brother would have helped you long ago, if we had been in a better position to do so. As you know, it was impossible. But now, if we make this proposal to our aunt, neither she nor Yasu will object. Stop worrying. I'm sure it will go through. I'll vouch for it.'

Receiving this assurance from Oyone, Koroku went out into the rain again and back to his lodging. He dropped by two days later to see if his brother had been to the Saekis yet. He came again three days after that. He had been to the Saekis himself and had learned that Sosuke had not yet been to see them. He urged Sosuke to go as soon as possible.

'I'll go, I'll go,' said Sosuke. Now it was full autumn. On a beautiful Sunday afternoon Sosuke, seeing that he was so late in calling on the Saekis, wrote them a letter explaining the plan for Koroku that he and Oyone had thought up. His aunt replied to this letter that Yasunosuke was away in Kobe.

54

V

It was on a Saturday afternoon a little after two o'clock that Mrs Saeki called on Sosuke. The skies had been unusually cloudy since morning and it was very cold. It seemed that the wind had suddenly shifted to the north. Mrs Saeki warmed her hands over a round brazier encased in bamboo and remarked to Oyone,

'This room is probably nice and cool in summer, but it must get very cold in winter.' Her naturally curly hair was done up neatly in a bun, and she wore a *haori*, tied in front with an old-fashioned cord. She was fond of sake and still took her measure with the evening meal each day. This may have been the reason why her face had such fine colour. Since she was also quite portly, she looked rather younger than she actually was. Whenever she came to visit them, Oyone would remark to her husband after she had gone,

'How young Auntie still looks.'

Sosuke would always reply, 'She ought to look young. After all, she's had only one child.'

Oyone agreed that this might account for her youthful appearance. But after such a conversation she would steal into the little room where her dressing-table was kept and take a look at her face in the mirror. It seemed to her that each time she looked, her cheeks were more sunken than before.

Nothing caused Oyone greater pain than to think of herself in relationship to children. At the landlord's house at the back there were a number of small children whose voices could be heard clearly as they played in the yard at the top of the cliff — swinging on their swings, playing hide-and-seek, and frolicking about in other games. Oyone, listening to them, would be filled with a feeling of emptiness and regret.

Her aunt, sitting there in front of her, had borne only one son, but she had done such a fine job in bringing him up and giving him an education that even now with her husband dead she had the look of one who lacks nothing. She was affluent enough, in fact, to sport a double chin. Yasunosuke was said to be constantly worried about her.

'Mother is overweight. If she doesn't take care, something may happen to her.'

To Oyone it seemed that both Yasunosuke, who was worried about his mother, and her aunt, who was the object of his worry, lived a very happy life together.

'Is Yasu back?' asked Oyone.

'Yes, he finally got back the night before last. I'm sorry we're so late in bringing you our answer.' But she did not indicate what that answer might be, and the conversation returned to Yasunosuke.

'He's finally graduated from college, but the next steps are the important ones. It's this I'm worried about. Still, he's been going to the factory in Tsukishima since September, and fortunately at this time it looks as if everything will continue to go well, if he applies himself properly. But he's very young. It's hard to know how much he'll change.'

Oyone broke in occasionally to exclaim, 'Oh, that's very fine,' or 'It's wonderful that everything's turned out so well.'

'His trip to Kobe too was on business for the company. He mentioned attaching a gas motor or something or other to a fishing boat.'

This meant nothing to Oyone and she merely said, 'Oh?'

Her aunt continued, 'I hadn't the slightest notion what he was talking about, and even after he'd explained it to me, all I could say was "Is that so?" I still don't know what a gas motor is,' and she laughed loudly.

'He says it's a machine that makes the boat move just by burning gasoline. To listen to him it's quite a wonderful thing. It saves the fishermen a lot of work. They can take the boat as far as ten or twenty miles out to sea with no trouble at all. And just think of the great number of fishing boats in Japan! If he can put one of these motors on each of them, he says he can make a tremendous profit. These days he's spending all his time and energy on this project. It's very nice to make a big profit, I keep telling him, but he mustn't become so taken up with his work that he neglects his health.'

Mrs Saeki talked away about fishing boats and Yasunosuke. She seemed to be very excited about the project herself. But she said not a word concerning Koroku. Sosuke, who should have been home long before, still did not make his appearance.

On his way back from work that day Sosuke got off the streetcar at Surugadai-shita and with a sour face walked two or three blocks to a dental clinic. Three or four days earlier when he was sitting talking to Oyone just before the evening meal, he happened to clamp his teeth firmly together, and he felt a sudden pain shoot through them. When he pressed a front tooth with his finger, its roots seemed to be unfirm. It was so sensitive that even the tea he drank with his meal and the air he breathed through his open mouth caused it to smart. That morning when he had brushed his teeth, he had carefully avoided the sensitive area. When he examined his mouth in a mirror, probing his teeth with a toothpick, two back teeth that he had had filled with silver in Hiroshima and an ill-assorted set of front teeth, worn down as if they had been filed, gleamed coldly back at him. As he changed into his office suit, he said,

'Oyone, this tooth looks pretty bad, doesn't it. It seems to be loose. When I press it like this, it gives,' and he demonstrated for her.

Oyone laughed and said, 'It's old age creeping on.' She moved behind him and fastened a white collar to his shirt.

That afternoon with firm resolve Sosuke finally called at the dentist. In the waiting-room was a large table surrounded by velvet-covered chairs, in which several people cowered, their chins buried in their collars. They were all

57

women. A handsome brown gas stove was still unlit. Sosuke sat and waited his turn, staring obliquely at the white walls reflected in a large mirror. Just as the waiting was becoming tedious, he noticed a pile of magazines on the table. He picked up a few and began to leaf through them. They were all women's magazines. He examined carefully the pictures of women that appeared in the rotogravure sections. Then he took up a magazine called *Success*. On its opening page was presented in outline the formula for success. One point of the summary stated that energetic drive was indispensable in everything. But, stated another, drive alone was not enough. To be effective, this drive must be directed towards a tenaciously held ideal. He read no further, but replaced the magazine. Success and Sosuke were poles apart. Until this minute he had not even known that there was a magazine with such a name. But no sooner had he put it down than he felt compelled to take it up again. This time his eye was caught by two lines of squarely-lettered characters written in classical Japanese.

The wind blows through the blue sky, chasing
away the clouds.
The moon climbs the eastern mountain, a brilliant
globe.

Sosuke had never been much interested in poetry. Still, for some reason or other these two lines appealed to him. It was not because they struck a nice counterpoint with each other, nor for any other reason of technique. Rather he suddenly felt that if a man could achieve an attitude of mind corresponding to the imagery of these two lines, he would be happy indeed. Out of curiosity he read through the article that preceded the verse, but it seemed to have no connection with it. Even after he had closed the magazine, the lines kept running through his mind. He realized how devoid of all lyricism his life of the past several years had been.

The door opposite him opened and the dentist's student-helper came out of the inner office and read out Sosuke's name from a slip of paper in his hand. Sosuke followed him into the treatment room.

The inner room was about twice as large as the waiting-room. It was designed to let in as much light as possible. Four dental chairs were ranged across the room with a dentist, clad in white, at each chair. Sosuke was shown to the chair farthest away from the door. He had to climb a kind of small step-ladder to get into it, and when he was settled, the helper gently tucked a heavy, striped cloth around him.

Now that he was peacefully reclining in the chair, Sosuke discovered that the tooth was giving him hardly any pain now. He noticed too that his shoulders, back, and hips were pleasantly relaxed, his whole body in a state of euphoria. He just lay there staring at the gas pipe coming down from the ceiling. It occurred to him that with this kind of service and equipment he would have to pay a higher fee than he had anticipated when he entered the clinic.

A fat man with a face too small for his features approached his chair and greeted him very politely. Startled out of his reverie, Sosuke lifted his head above the chair and nodded a greeting in return. The fat man asked what was wrong and began to examine his mouth, pushing a little on the aching tooth.

'I'm afraid that if it gives like this, it'll be impossible to make it as firm again as it was before. The core seems to be dead.' To Sosuke these words evoked an image of the melancholy light of autumn. He wanted to ask if he had already reached such an age, but he was too embarrassed to do so, and he said only, as if for confirmation,

'Then it won't get better?'

The fat man laughed and answered, 'I wish I could tell you that it will, but the fact is that it won't. When it gets too bad, we can pull it. But it hasn't reached that stage yet, so I'll just do something about the pain. Necrosis has set in . . . you probably don't know what that means. It's as if the core of the tooth were rotten.'

Sosuke said only, 'Is that so?' and let the fat man do as he liked with the tooth. The dentist started his drill and began to drill a hole at the root of the tooth. Then he injected something like a long needle into the hole. Finally he pulled out what looked like a piece of thread.

'I've taken out this much nerve,' he said, showing the cut nerve to Sosuke. He dabbed medicine into the hole and told him to come back again the following day.

When Sosuke got out of the chair, his line of vision, now that his body was vertical again, moved suddenly from the ceiling to the garden. A large potted pine-tree about five feet high caught his eye. A gardener wearing straw sandals was carefully wrapping straw matting about the base of the tree. It was the season, Sosuke reflected, when the dew gradually began to freeze and turn into frost, when those who could afford to do so began to make preparations against the oncoming winter.

On the way out he stopped at the drug counter and received some gargling powder, with the instructions to dissolve a small amount in lukewarm water and gargle ten time a day. Then he stopped to pay the treatment fee and rejoiced to see that it was really very modest. At this rate it would be no great strain on his finances to come back four or five times as he had been told to do. When he bent down to put on his shoes, he noticed that the soles were in poor condition.

He reached home shortly after his aunt had made her departure.

'She was here, was she?' he said, as he changed his clothes, which today seemed to be something of a chore. He took his place as usual in front of the brazier. Oyone picked up his shirt, trousers, and socks in one armful and carried them into the next room. Relaxed now, he began to smoke. He could hear the sound of Oyone's clothes-

60

brush as she brushed his suit, and he called out to her,

'Oyone, did she have anything to say?'

Now that the pain in his tooth had subsided, the cold feeling of being oppressed by autumn was also somewhat alleviated. He had Oyone take the gargling medicine out of his pocket and dissolve a portion of it in lukewarm water, and he began to gargle vigorously. Then stepping on to the veranda, he remarked to his wife ,

'The days have become short.'

Soon it was dark. Even during the day few sounds from the street found their way here, but now at night it was perfectly still. Husband and wife took their usual places beside the lamp. It seemed to them that in this wide world only the place where they sat was light. And in this circle of light Sosuke was conscious only of Oyone, and Oyone only of Sosuke. They forgot all about the dark world which the light of their lamp did not illumine. Spending all their evenings in this way, they had come to discover their own life.

Silently the couple regarded the present that Yasunosuke had brought back from Kobe for them. It was a special kind of spiced seaweed. The can rattled when shaken. They opened it and took out a few pieces, then leisurely discussed the answer their aunt had brought to their proposal.

'But she should be able to find some way of taking care of at least his tuition and spending money.'

'That's exactly what she says she can't do. Added up, the total figure would come to about ten yen. She says she would be very hard put to it under present circumstances to pay that much regularly every month.'

'Then it must be just as hard to get together the twenty yen needed to take care of him till the end of the year.'

'She says it is, but that they can manage somehow or other for these two months. After that, she says, Yasu wants us to make some other provision.'

'I wonder if they're really that hard-pressed.'

61

'I don't know. But that's what she says.'

'If they're making so much money on fishing boats, you'd think this would be a simple matter for them.'

'Yes, that's true.'

Oyone laughed in a low voice. Sosuke also moved his lips slightly but the laugh did not come. There was a long pause, and then Sosuke said,

'At any rate, we have no choice but to take Koroku in. All planning must begin at that point. He's still going to school, I suppose.'

'I believe so.'

Sosuke rose abruptly, walked to his small study, and shut himself in it, something he had not done for a long time. When Oyone quietly opened the door and looked in an hour later, he was sitting before his desk engrossed in a book.

'You're studying? Hadn't you better get to bed?'

He looked around at her and said, 'Yes, let's go to bed,' and followed her out of the room. He took off his *yukata* and put on his *nemaki*. As he wound the sash about his waist, he said,

'Tonight I read Confucius' *Analects* for the first time in a long while.'

'Did you find anything there?'

'No, nothing.' Then he added, 'As I thought, the trouble with my teeth is age. That's what the dentist said. There's nothing that can be done to prevent their coming loose.' Then he laid his dark head on the pillow.

VI

It was decided in consultation with Koroku that whenever it was convenient for him he should leave his present lodging and move in with his brother. Oyone looked regretfully at the mulberry dressing-table in the room Koroku would occupy, and said somewhat plaintively to Sosuke.

'We'll be cramped for space, won't we?' Now that she had to give up this room, she was left without a place to make her toilet.

Sosuke had no words to console her. He rose and looked obliquely into the mirror placed next to the window on the other side of the room. From that angle he saw one side of Oyone's face reflected in the glass. He was surprised to see how pale she looked.

'Is something wrong? Your colour's very bad.' He moved his eyes from the mirror to Oyone herself. Her hair was in disorder and the back of her neck looked dirty.

Oyone answered only, 'It must be the cold,' and she opened the doors of the closet on the western side of the room. At the bottom was an old scarred chest of drawers, and on top of it were piled a brief case and several willow hampers.

'There's no place to put these things.'

'Then why don't you leave them where they are?'

From the point of view of space Koroku's moving into the house was something of an inconvenience to both of them. For that reason, when Koroku, after promising to come to live with them, was slow in making his appearance, they urged him no further. Without putting it into words, both felt that even one day's postponement saved them from that much inconvenience. Koroku, meanwhile, had the same hesitation in abandoning his convenient lodging, and he postponed his departure day after day, as if he had set his mind on staying where he was as long as he possibly could. But unlike Sosuke and Oyone he was by nature unable to find peace of mind when everything was up in the air like this.

Meanwhile the frost had settled on to the garden and had wilted the branches of the Basho tree at the back. Every morning the shrill peeps of little chicks could be heard from the direction of the landlord's garden at the top of the cliff, and in the evening the sound of the wooden gong of Enmyoji Temple mingled with the horn of the *tofu* vendor as he hurried along his rounds on the street in front. The days became shorter and shorter. Oyone's colour had not improved from the day Sosuke had caught her reflection in the mirror. Several times Sosuke found her in bed taking a nap when he returned home from work. When he asked if anything was wrong, she replied only that she was slightly under the weather. He proposed calling in a doctor, but she objected, saying that she was not that ill.

Sosuke was worried. Even at the office he had Oyone on his mind — to the point of its interfering with his work, he realized. But one day in the streetcar on his way home, a light suddenly dawned on him. That afternoon he was in unusually good spirits as he entered the house. He rushed immediately to Oyone's side and asked how she was feeling today. Oyone, as usual, gathered up the clothes he had just removed and went into the next room to put them away. He followed her.

'Oyone, could it be that you're pregnant?' he asked, laughing. Oyone gave no answer, but with downcast eyes kept on brushing vigorously at the jacket of her husband's suit. Even after the sound of the brush had stopped, she still did not come out. Sosuke re-entered the room to see what she was doing. She was sitting in front of the mirror in the cold and fast darkening room. She answered his call in a voice that sounded as if she had been crying.

That evening the two sat opposite each other, holding their hands over the tea-kettle set on the brazier.

'What's happening in the world?' Sosuke asked in an

unusually cheerful voice. The image of Sosuke and herself as they had been before their marriage came vividly to Oyone's mind.

'Let's go out and have a little fun. We've been living in too gloomy an atmosphere recently,' said Sosuke, and the two began to make plans to go somewhere together the following Sunday. After some time the conversation turned to the subject of spring clothes. Sosuke told Oyone of the wife of one of his fellow workers, a man by the name of Takagi, who had begged her husband to buy her a new coat. But the husband had refused, saying that he was not working every day just to satisfy his wife's vanity. The wife, upset at this refusal, had defended herself. In this cold weather, she protested, she had nothing to wear outside the house. In that case, replied the husband, she could always wrap a quilt about her shoulders or put a blanket over her head when she went out, but that for the time being she would have to do with what she had. Sosuke gave such a funny account of the incident that Oyone couldn't help laughing. Seeing her husband in such good humour, Oyone felt as if the past had for the moment returned.

'Takagi's wife may very well do with just a quilt, but I was thinking that I'd like a new overcoat myself. The other day at the dentist's I saw a gardener tucking straw around the roots of some dwarf pines, and I suddenly felt I wanted a new overcoat.'

'You'd like to buy a new overcoat?'

'Yes.'

There was sympathy in the look Oyone gave her husband as she said, 'Then go ahead and buy one. We can always pay for it in instalments.'

But Sosuke suddenly changed his mind, and said in a cheerless voice, 'I suppose I don't really need one.' Then he changed the subject.

'I wonder when Koroku is planning to move in.'

'He probably hasn't much heart for coming,' answered

Oyone. From the beginning she had felt that Koroku did not like her. But since he was her husband's brother, she had done her best to get on well with him and to close the distance between them. In this she had succeeded and she believed that they were now on as familiar terms as a wife generally becomes with her brother-in-law. Still, when something like this came up, her suspicions were again aroused, and, rushing beyond fact, convinced her that she was the reason Koroku hesitated in coming.

'I can understand why he is reluctant to exchange his present lodging for a place like this. After all, just as we feel the inconvenience of having him move in, so he must feel the inconvenience of being cooped up here with us. But if he doesn't come, I'm going to go right ahead and have that coat made at once.'

Sosuke spoke out with a virile decisiveness. But his words were not enough to dispel the cloud over Oyone's heart. She made no answer but remained silent for a time. With her slender chin tucked into the collar of her kimono, she looked up and said finally,

'I wonder if Koroku doesn't still hate me.' Since coming to Tokyo she had occasionally given voice to such apprehensions, and each time Sosuke had done his best to reassure her. But of late she had made no further mention of it and he thought she had got over her doubts, and he had forgotten about them himself.

'Your imagination's running away with you again. Besides, what does it matter what Koroku thinks . . . as long as I'm around?'

'Did you find that in Confucius?'

Oyone was the kind of woman who could make a joke at a time like this.

'Yes, I certainly did,' Sosuke answered, and the conversation ended there.

The next morning when Sosuke awoke, he heard a chilling sound on the zinc roof above him. Oyone appeared at his pillow, her sleeves already tucked up for the day's housework.

'It's time to get up.'

Listening to the rain beating down on the roof, he would have liked to enjoy the warmth of his bed for a while longer, but seeing Oyone already up and about, her face as pale as ever, he jumped out at once.

The view outside was obstructed by the heavy downpour. The bamboos at the top of the cliff swung their manes to and fro, as if to shake off the rain. All that could fortify Sosuke for venturing out to be soaked in this miserable weather was a breakfast of hot *misoshiru* and rice.

'My shoes will be wet through and through again. It's really hard to do without two pairs.' But since there was nothing to be done about it, he put on his shoes with the soles worn through in several places, and rolled up his trouser legs.

When he returned in the afternoon, Oyone had placed a pail with rags to absorb the raindrops near the dressing-table of the room that was to be Koroku's. The portion of ceiling immediately above the pail was discoloured, and every few seconds a drop of water trickled down.

'It's not only the inside of my shoes. Even the inside of the house is wet,' said Sosuke, smiling wryly. That evening Oyone put some hot coals into a foot-warmer and dried her husband's socks and trousers over it.

Rain fell again the following day. Sosuke and Oyone went through the same routine as the day before. Nor were the skies clear even on the day after that. On the morning of the third day Sosuke knitted his eyebrows and said with disgust,

'How long does it intend to go on raining? The insides of my shoes are so wet that I can hardly bear to put them on.'

'Koroku's room is a mess too. The roof is really leaking now.'

The upshot of this conversation was that they decided to ask the landlord to repair the leaking roof. But there was nothing to be done about the shoes. Sosuke forced his feet into them and listened to them squeak as he walked off to work.

Fortunately the weather cleared up about eleven o'clock to become a beautiful, spring-like day with sparrows chirping in the hedges, and when Sosuke returned home from work that evening, even Oyone had a healthier complexion than usual.

'Sosuke, we couldn't sell that folding screen?' she asked suddenly. The screen painted by Hoitsu had remained in a corner of the study ever since the day the Saekis had sent it to them. It had only two panels, but because of the size and arrangement of their parlour, it was a useless decoration that only got in the way. If they placed it against the southern wall, it covered half of the entrance from the front vestibule. If they moved it around to the eastern side, it cut off the light coming into the room; and if they placed it on the northern side, it concealed the *tokonoma*. Finally even Sosuke had to admit,

'I accepted the screen from the Saekis thinking it would put me in mind of my father, but it's really just a worthless space filler.'

While he spoke, Oyone looked at the round silver moon with the scorched edge and the stalks of *susuki* grass, which had the texture of silk, and she seemed quite unable to understand how anyone could place any value on such a work. But in deference to her husband, she had never put her feeling into words. Once only she had said, 'And this is supposed to be a fine painting?' On that occasion Sosuke had told her for the first time about Hoitsu. His explanation was nothing more than a general and rather vague recounting of what he himself remembered having heard from his father long before. When it came to the actual value of the painting or the detailed history of Hoitsu, Sosuke himself had only a vague recollection.

Sosuke's explanation unexpectedly motivated Oyone to what for her was a very unusual action. A week after the above conversation she recalled her husband's words and had a very happy thought. It was the day the skies cleared, and the sun was once again streaming into the house. She put on her coat, and without bothering about either a shawl or even a scarf, rushed out of the house. She walked about two blocks down the street, turned in the direction of the streetcar tracks, and kept on walking until she came to a cluster of shops, where between a grocery store and a bakery there was to be found a shop that sold second-hand goods and antiques. Oyone remembered having bought a folding table here once. The tea-kettle which sat on their charcoal brazier had also been bought by Sosuke one day at this shop.

Oyone stood in front for a time looking in, her hands thrust into the sleeves of her *haori* for warmth. As always, a large number of new tea-kettles were lined up on the shelves. What caught her eye next, after the tea-kettles, were the charcoal braziers, also in large quantity, a display appropriate to the season. But she couldn't find anything within that rated the title of 'antique'. An extraordinarily large tortoise shell was hanging on the back wall, and a long yellow streamer fell down from it, looking very much like the tortoise's tail. One or two rosewood tea-shelves were on display, but the wood looked so green still that there was every possibility of its warping. Oyone, however, had no eye to discern this. After standing there long enough to ascertain that there was not a single *kakemono* or folding screen to be seen in the shop, she walked in.

She had come, of course, to see about the possibility of selling the screen Sosuke had received from his aunt. She felt none of the hesitation or uneasiness of the usual house-wife in such a situation, since she had come to have con-

69

siderable experience of second-hand stores from the time they had lived in Hiroshima. She could walk up with resolve to the owner of the shop and begin negotiations with him.

He was a man of about fifty, with puffy cheeks, swarthy complexion and wearing huge horn-rimmed glasses. He was sitting reading a newspaper over an iron brazier speckled with wart-like blemishes.

In reply to Oyone's query, he said, 'I suppose I could go over and have a look at it.' Oyone was somewhat disheartened at his lack of enthusiasm. Since, however, she had not from the first entertained much hope of success, she was content to have him come to see it, even if it meant that she placed herself at the disadvantage of seeming more eager to sell than he was to buy.

'Fine. I'll be around later. Right now I'm all alone in the shop.'

With this casual answer, Oyone returned home, but she seriously doubted if he would ever come to see the screen. She had her usual simple midday meal and was just instructing Kiyo to clear away the table when the man from the shop appeared at the door. She let him into the house and showed him the the screen. He examined it carefully, but noncommittally, and finally, after a little thought, named a price.

'I'll give you six yen for it.'

Oyone had not expected much more. All the same, she thought it better to wait and discuss the matter with her husband first. Besides, the screen did have a considerable sentimental value for him, and this made her hesitate all the more. She told the man she would talk it over with Sosuke and let him know. He prepared to leave, but on his way out he said,

'All right, then. I'll give you seven yen for it. Will you sell it for that?'

'But, after all, it's a Hoitsu,' Oyone summoned up the

courage to say, aware at the same time of a chill at the pit of her stomach.

The man was not impressed. 'Hoitsu is not very popular these days.' He looked for a long time at Oyone. As he turned to leave, he said, 'Talk it over with your husband and let me know what you decide.'

After Oyone had explained everything to Sosuke, she asked innocently, 'Wouldn't it be all right to sell it?'

For some time Sosuke had been trying to think of a way to raise their standard of living. But he and his wife had grown so accustomed to their simple life that they were now quite resigned to making an inadequate income adequate. Thus he made no effort to supplement his meagre wages so that they might be able to lead a more leisurely life. His reaction upon hearing of Oyone's plan to sell the screen was one of surprise at her good sense. All the same, he wondered if it was really necessary to go so far. When he asked what she herself thought about it, she explained that with the money he could have the new shoes he needed and she could buy material for a dress. That was true, thought Sosuke, but when he weighed the screen of Hoitsu, that had been handed down to him from his father, against the new shoes and material for a dress, it seemed a fantastic, even ludicrous, exchange.

'If you want to sell it, go ahead and do so. After all, it only gets in the way here. But I can still get along for a while with the shoes I have. Of course, if we have another spell of rainy weather like the last, I'll be in trouble. But the weather's turned fine now.'

'If it starts raining again, you'll have to get new shoes.'

Sosuke could not very well assure Oyone that the weather would always be fine, and Oyone on her part could not bring herself to urge him to sell the screen before the next rainfall. The two looked at each other and laughed. Finally Oyone asked,

'Is the price too low?'

71

'Yes, I think so.'

When asked for his opinion, the price did seem to him to be insufficient. He felt that if there were indeed a buyer for the screen, he wanted to get whatever that buyer was willing to pay for it. He thought he had read in the newspaper that old *kakemono* were now selling at a very good price. If only he still had at least one in his possession! But these were now all out of his reach. It was no use thinking about it.

'I suppose it depends on the buyer. And, of course, it depends on the seller too. However fine a work the screen may be, it's hardly likely that anyone would offer us a very high price for it. Still, seven or eight yen seems much too little.'

Sosuke's words showed that at the same time as he defended the value of the screen, he could also understand the position of the dealer. Only for himself, he felt, was it impossible to offer excuses. Oyone had not the heart to urge the matter further.

The next day at the office Sosuke told everyone about the screen and the price offered for it. All agreed that it was much too little. But no one volunteered to take it upon himself to find a buyer willing to pay what the screen was worth, nor did anyone even suggest how to go about disposing of it so as to get its full value. Sosuke had no alternative but to sell it to the owner of the second-hand shop. Otherwise it would just remain standing in their little home, getting in their way.

Sosuke placed it in the parlour, where it had originally stood, and the dealer came again. This time he offered fifteen yen for it. Sosuke and Oyone exchanged glances and smiled. They decided to hold on to it for a while longer. The dealer came a third time. This time too they refused to sell. Even Oyone found it pleasing to refuse. On his fourth visit the dealer brought along a man they had never seen before. The two consulted together in a low voice and finally came up with the figure of thirty-five yen. Then Sosuke and Oyone talked it over on the spot and made the decision to sell.

VII

The cryptomeria trees of Enmyoji Temple were a reddish-black, as if they had been scorched. On nice days a white line of mountains rose up steeply against a corner of sky washed by the wind. The year plunged ahead, driving Sosuke and his wife day by day into ever greater cold and discomfort. In the morning the call of the *natto* vendor, who never failed to make his round, put them in mind of frost on roof-tiles. Listening to his call from the warmth of bed, Sosuke reflected that it was indeed winter again. In the kitchen Oyone had begun to experience the inconveniences that marked the passage from the end of the year to spring. She hoped that this winter the water would not freeze in the pipes as it had the winter before. At night the couple sat together in the *kotatsu,* enjoying each other's company and recalling with nostalgia the warmer winters of Hiroshima and Fukuoka.

'We've become just like the Hondas, haven't we?' Oyone said laughing. The Hondas were the retired couple living next door in another house owned by their landlord, Mr Sakai. With their one maid, they lived so quietly that hardly a sound was to be heard there from morning to night. When Oyone was sewing alone in the parlour, she occasionally heard someone next door call 'Grandpa, grandpa.' It was the voice of Mrs Honda calling her husband. And when Oyone chanced to meet her going in or coming out of the house, they would exchange greetings, generally little more than commentary on the weather. Mrs Honda would invite Oyone to come over some time for a chat, but Oyone had never taken her up on it, and Mrs Honda for her part had never set foot in Oyone's house. In short, Sosuke and Oyone knew very little about the Hondas. They had heard from a delivery boy from one of the stores in the neighbourhood that the Hondas had one son, who held a very fine position as a public official in Korea and who sent enough each month to enable them to live quite comfortably. But this was all they knew.

'Is the old man still fussing over his plants?'

'Probably not. It's getting too cold. He has many pots lined up under the veranda.'

The conversation turned from the Hondas to Mr Sakai, the landlord. The latter was the exact opposite of the Hondas, and it seemed to Sosuke and Oyone that there could not be another family so full of life and good cheer. Their back yard at the top of the cliff had taken on the cold and grey of winter, and children no longer frolicked there as in summer. Instead, a piano could be heard almost every evening. Occasionally even the shrill laughter of the maid in the kitchen reached them as they sat in their parlour.

'What is his occupation?' asked Sosuke. He had already put this question to his wife several times.

'I don't think he has an occupation. He just takes things easy . . . living off the income of his land and houses.' Oyone gave him the same answer she had given him before.

Sosuke never carried his inquiry further. When he had broken off his schooling, he had felt like warning everyone he met who seemed to bask in fortune's smile to look out for the future. After a time this feeling had turned into outright hatred of those more fortunate than himself. Still later, he came to be possessed by a sense of the deep chasm that separates self and other. He came to see himself now as one born to be uniquely himself, with a destiny peculiarly his own. Self and others were from the start distinct categories, with human nature all that was held in common. There could be no commerce or influence for good or evil between them. Occasionally when making small talk, he might ask what so-and-so did for a living, but it was too much bother to pursue the matter further. Oyone felt very much the same as he did. But this evening she did something unprecedented and gave her husband detailed information about the Sakais. Mr Sakai was without a beard and looked about forty. The girl who played the piano was his eldest daughter, a girl of about twelve or thirteen. When children from other houses came to play, they were not allowed to use the swings.

'Why doesn't he let the other children play on the swings?'

'Because he's stingy, I suppose. He's afraid they'll wear out and have to be replaced.'

Sosuke laughed. It would surely be a contradiction, he thought, for a landlord as stingy as Sakai to supply the tiles to repair a leaking roof or call a gardener to replace the dead shrubbery in the hedge.

That night Sosuke dreamt neither of Honda and his pots nor of Sakai and his swings. He went to bed about ten-thirty and began to snore like a man completely exhausted. Oyone, who had been having headaches recently and consequently found it hard to get to sleep, opened her eyes from time to time and looked about the dark room. A slender flame was visible in the *tokonoma*. They were accustomed to keep a light burning all night. When they went to bed, they lowered the wick of the lamp and placed it in the *tokonoma*.

Oyone kept changing the position of her pillow, as if she couldn't find the just the right place. Each time she did so, her lower shoulder would slip out of the covers. Finally, lying flat on her stomach and propping herself up on her elbows, she looked over at her husband for some time. Then, getting out of bed, she put over her nightgown the kimono that had been thrown over the foot of the bed, and took up the lamp.

Coming close to her husband's pillow, she squatted beside him and called, 'Sosuke, Sosuke!' He stopped snoring and his breathing became that of one who is in deep sleep. She stood up, lamp in hand, opened the door to the *chanoma*, and stepped in. When the darkness of the room had been slightly dispelled by the feeble light of her small lamp, the metal rings of the chest of drawers shone with a dull glow. Passing through this room into the smoke-blackened kitchen, she could make out only the white of the cupboard doors. She stood there for a while in the cold kitchen, then noiselessly opened the door to the adjacent room, which was the maid's, and shone her lamp inside. Under the bedclothes, the pattern and colour of which could not be made out clearly in the dim light, the maid was curled up like a mole, asleep. She looked next into the small room on the other side of the kitchen. It was empty except for her dressing-table. Her eye was caught and held by the mirror, the more so for its being night.

After she had made a complete round of the house and had satisfied herself that all was well, Oyone returned to bed and closed her eyes finally. Now, happily, she felt no further nervous pressure about her eyelids and was able to get to sleep at once.

No sooner had she fallen asleep than she woke again with a start. She thought she had heard a heavy thud beside her pillow. Raising her head, she tried to figure out what it might have been. All she could think of was that a large, heavy object had come rolling down the embankment at the back of the house to the edge of the veranda of the room where they slept. Moreover, it must have happened just the moment before she opened her eyes. It could not have been just a dream. She was suddenly afraid, and pulling at her husband asleep beside her, she tried to wake him.

Sosuke had been sound asleep, but thus abruptly awakened by Oyone pleading with him to get up, he rose quickly from the covers, still half as if in a dream. Oyone explained in a low voice what she had heard.

'Did you hear the sound only once?'

'Yes, but it was just a moment ago.'

The two were silent, listening, their ears attuned to the darkness outside. But everything was still. However long they waited with ears pricked, the sound as of something falling did not repeat itself. 'It's cold,' said Sosuke, and he put on a coat over his night clothes, rolled back one of the *amado*, stepped out on to the veranda, and peered into the darkness. But there was nothing to be seen. Only a blast of cold air came suddenly out of the dark to assault him. Sosuke closed the *amado* in a hurry, returned to the room, and crawled quickly under the bedclothes.

'I couldn't find anything. You probably dreamt it,' he said, as he stretched himself out. Oyone insisted that it had not been a dream, that she had really heard a heavy thud over her head. Sosuke turned his face, which was only half-way out of the covers, towards Oyone and said,

'Oyone, your nerves are on edge. You're not well these days. You've got to give your head a rest and find a way to get more sleep at night.'

Just then the wall clock in the next room struck two. At the sound, the couple broke off their conversation and fell quiet. The night seemed shrouded in even deeper silence than before. The eyes of both were wide open and refused to close in sleep.

'You've got nothing on your mind. You fall asleep within ten minutes of lying down,' said Oyone.

'I fall asleep all right, but it's not because there's nothing on my mind. It's just that I'm tired enough to sleep,' answered Sosuke.

In the middle of this conversation Sosuke fell asleep again. Oyone, however, kept tossing and turning as before. She heard a cart pass outside, making a terrible noise. Several times of late she had been surprised to hear a cart

77

pass just before dawn. It was always at this same time, and she surmised that it must be the same one, perhaps the milkman on his rounds. At any rate, the sound told her it was dawn and that people about her had already begun the day's activity, and it made her feel good. Then from somewhere she heard a cock crow, followed by the clatter of *geta* in the street.

Soon after, she heard Kiyo open the door of her room and go to the toilet, then enter the room next to hers, perhaps to see what time it was. By now the oil of the lamp in the *tokonoma* was too low to reach the short wick, and the room was pitch black, so that the light in Kiyo's hand cast its rays through the cracks of the sliding doors that separated the two rooms.

'Kiyo?' Oyone called.

Kiyo returned to bed, but rose again soon afterwards. Half an hour later Oyone rose, and after another half hour, Sosuke. Oyone always called him when it was time to get up. 'You can get up now' were her usual words. On Sundays and the rare holidays this became 'Please get up now'. But today, perhaps because he had Oyone's fears of the night before still in mind, he got out of bed before her call, quickly rolled back the *amado* on the side of the room facing the cliff, and looked up.

Behind the bamboos, which seemed to be immobilized by the cold morning air, the rising sun melted the frost and coloured slightly the top of the embankment. Sosuke was surprised to see that the withered stalks of grass at the steepest point of the incline were damaged and that raw red clay was exposed at their roots. Letting his eyes follow a direct line downwards, he saw that the ground immediately below the edge of the veranda on which he stood was disturbed and the frost patterns broken. He wondered if something like a big dog could possibly have come rolling down from the top. But on second thoughts, no dog, however big, would have landed with such an impact.

78

Sosuke got his *geta* from the front entrance and stepped into the yard. Since the toilet jutted out at an angle from the veranda, there was only a very narrow passage between the house and the cliff. Whenever the man came to take away the rubbish, Oyone would point out the passage apprehensively and say, 'If there were a little more room here!' Sosuke only laughed at her fears.

Beyond this passage was a narrow path leading to the kitchen. There had been a cryptomeria hedge with many dead branches separating Sosuke's yard from the one next door, but only recently the landlord had pulled up the hedge, with its yawning gaps, and replaced it with a wooden fence, full of knots, extending all the way to the kitchen entrance. This side of the house got very little sun and the soil was watered by the rain that dripped down from the eaves. The plot was full of begonias in summer. At the height of their season the green leaves laced together so luxuriantly as to leave very little trace of a path. The sight had been enough to astonish Sosuke and Oyone the first summer they had seen it. These begonias had crept along the ground here for years and had continued to do so even after the old house that had stood on the site had been torn down. When the season arrived they would send out their buds as they had in the past, and could still elicit from Oyone an exclamation of joy at their beauty.

Sosuke left his footprints on the frost-covered ground as he made his way to the other side, cold and untouched by the sun, but even now full of memories of summer's begonias. Suddenly his eye darted to a spot on the narrow path and he stopped in his tracks. There ahead of him lay a gold lacquer letter-box. It was set squarely in the centre of the frosted path, as if someone had purposely brought it to this spot and abandoned it. Near it was the lid, thrown up against the fence, upside-down, the pattern of its decorative paper lining clearly visible. Letters and other papers that had been kept in the box were scattered everywhere.

Among them one rather long letter had been unfolded to a length of two feet and the rest crumpled into a ball like so much waste paper. After closer inspection Sosuke smiled wryly. Under the crushed paper lay human faeces.

He gathered together the scattered documents, replaced them in the letter-box, and brought the box, wet and grimy as it was, to the kitchen entrance. Opening the door, he called to Kiyo.

'Here, please take this,' and he handed the letter-box to her. Kiyo had a wondering look on her face as she took it from him. Oyone was cleaning in the parlour. Sosuke continued his round of the house all the way to the front gate, but he found nothing else disturbed.

Finally he went back into the house. He entered the *chanoma* and took his usual place in front of the brazier. He called Oyone in a loud voice.

'Where did you go off to as soon as you got up?' she asked as she entered the room.

'That sound you said you heard last night — it wasn't a dream after all. It was a thief. It was the sound of a thief tumbling down from Sakai's place at the top all the way into our yard. Just now when I walked round the back, I found this letter-box on the ground and letters and papers scattered all over the place. For good measure, the thief had left his perfumed visiting card on one of the letters.'

Sosuke took two or three letters out of the box and showed them to Oyone. They were all addressed to Mr Sakai. Oyone was surprised.

'I wonder if anything else was stolen.'

'I suppose it's quite possible,' Sosuke answered, folding his arms.

The two left the letter-box beside the brazier and sat down to breakfast. But even during the meal they continued to discuss the theft. Oyone boasted to her husband that even when asleep her mind and ears stood guard. He replied that he was happy that his did not.

'That's what you say. But suppose the thief had tried to break in here instead of at Sakai's. A deep sleeper like you wouldn't have known anything about it,' Oyone countered.

'What are you saying? No need to worry about a thief breaking in here.' Sosuke would not let his wife have the last word.

Kiyo suddenly stuck her head out of the kitchen and exclaimed joyfully, 'Aren't we lucky the thief picked on Sakai and not on us! Imagine if he'd broken in here and stolen the new coat you made for the master the other day.' She spoke with such seriousness that Sosuke and Oyone were momentarily at a loss for an answer.

After breakfast there was still a good bit of time left before starting for work. Since Sakai must surely be greatly disturbed about the theft, Sosuke decided to take the letter-box up to him at once. It was a lacquer box, but a very plain one, with a tortoise-shell pattern embossed in gold on black. It did not seem to be of much value. Oyone wrapped it up for him in a cloth. Since the cloth was just a little small for the box, she knotted the four corners together. When Sosuke took it up, it looked like a gift box of cakes.

Sakai's home was immediately overhead, but to approach it from the front it was necessary to walk half a block down the street, climb the slope, then return half a block. Sosuke walked along a neat hedge of Chinese hawthorn, beyond which extended a strip of lawn studded with garden stones, until he came to Sakai's entrance.

Contrary to what he had expected, there was no sign of excitement within. Everything was still, almost too still. Reaching the front door, which had frosted glass windows, he rang the doorbell two or three times, but it didn't seem to be working. At least, no one came to the door. There was nothing for him to do but go round to the kitchen entrance. There too the door had a frosted glass window. He could hear someone rattling dishes inside. He opened the door and called out a greeting to a maid who was squatting beside a little gas cooking-burner.

'I wonder if this belongs to Mr Sakai. I found it this morning in my back yard and brought it over,' he said, holding out the letter-box.

The maid thanked him simply and took the letter-box. Going to the entrance to the next room, she called another maid and handed the box to her, with a few words of explanation in a low voice. The second maid looked towards Sosuke as she took the box, but disappeared immediately into the next room. Just then a girl of about twelve or thirteen with a round face and large eyes and a younger girl who seemed to be her sister — they wore identical ribbons in their hair — popped into the kitchen and began whispering to each other, their eyes fixed on Sosuke. Sosuke caught only the one word 'thief'. Having handed over the letter-box, he considered his purpose accomplished and made a move to leave, not waiting for any further word from inside.

But before leaving, just to make certain, he asked again, 'The letter-box does belong here, doesn't it?' The kitchen maid, who obviously knew nothing about it, was at a loss for an answer, when the second maid reappeared.

'Won't you please step inside,' she said politely, bowing. Now it was Sosuke's turn to be embarrassed. As he stood hesitating, she repeated her invitation, even more politely than before. His feeling of embarrassment began to give way to one of annoyance. At that point Sakai himself entered the room.

As Sosuke had imagined, he was a man of ruddy complexion and plump cheeks and with an air of prosperity about him. But Oyone had been wrong in one thing. He did have a beard. It began below the nose as a shortly clipped moustache and extended neatly across to his cheeks and circled his chin.

'You've gone to a lot of trouble. Thank you.' Wrinkles

gathered at the corners of his eyes as he expressed his thanks. Without haste he questioned Sosuke about his find. Sosuke summarized briefly the events of the previous night and the morning, and then asked if anything else had been stolen. Sakai replied that a gold watch, which he had left on his desk, had also been taken. He did not seem to be the least disturbed about the theft and spoke as unemotionally as if the objects stolen had belonged to somebody else. He was more interested in Sosuke's story than in the watch. He wondered if the thief had planned to escape through the back and make his way down the embankment, or if perhaps in his rush to get away he had actually fallen down it. Sosuke could not answer.

The first maid entered the room with tea and tobacco, and Sosuke's departure was still further delayed. Sakai pulled out a cushion and invited Sosuke to sit down and have tea with him. Then he told Sosuke what the detective, who had come early that morning, had conjectured. He surmised that the thief had sneaked into the grounds in the early evening and hidden himself in a shed until the family were asleep. He must have got into the house through the kitchen door. He struck a match, lit a candle and stood it inside a small wooden bucket he found in the kitchen, and made his way from there to the *chanoma*. Since Mrs Sakai and the children were sleeping in the next room, he followed the corridor to Mr Sakai's study. But while he was rummaging in there the baby, just a few days old, woke and began to cry. At the sound, the thief must have been startled and made a quick escape through the door of the study out into the garden.

'If only the dog had been here as usual to receive him! Unfortunately, he took ill and we had to send him to the vet a few days ago,' stated Sakai regretfully.

'That's too bad,' agreed Sosuke.

Then Sakai began to explain about the dog's breed and

pedigree and how he sometimes took him out hunting. And he went on talking.

'I like to hunt. Of course, I've been suffering for some time from a nervous disorder and I've had to take things easy. Still, from the beginning of autumn until winter I go snipe shooting. For two or three hours I stay standing in mud almost up to my hips. I suppose that's not very good for one's health.'

Sakai seemed to have limitless time at his disposal. Sosuke had only to give a perfunctory response and he was off again, talking on and on with no sign of stopping. Finally Sosuke had to rise while he was still talking and make his apologies.

'Since I have to go to work today as usual. . . .' Only then did Sakai break off his chatter and apologize for having detained him so long when he was very busy. The detective, he added, would probably want to have a look at the place where the box had been found. He apologized in advance for the trouble.

As Sosuke was leaving, he said politely, 'I haven't much to do these days, so I'll be able to call on you.' Sosuke went out of the gate and hurried home. It was already half an hour later than the time he usually set out for work.

Oyone came out of the house with a worried expression. 'What kept you so long?' As he quickly changed into his business suit, he remarked to her, 'That Sakai is certainly an easy-going fellow. I suppose if a person has money he can afford to take things easy.'

VIII

'Koroku, how about beginning with the *chanoma,* or else with the parlour?' said Oyone.

Koroku had finally moved in a few days before, and to-day it was his job to help Oyone change the paper of the *shoji*. While he was still living with his uncle, he and Yasu-nosuke had once repapered the *shoji* of his own room. He had mixed the paste and spread it over the frame with a spatula, all very professionally. Everything went well until the paper dried and he tried to put the *shoji* back in place. He could not fit the two panels together into their grooves. He and Yasu had failed a second time at the same task. Asked by his aunt to repaper the *shoji* of the house, they had made the mistake of soaking the frames in water to remove the old paper. The frames warped in drying and that time too they had trouble getting them back in place.

'Oyone, unless you're careful, you can really make a mess of this . . . especially if you try to wash off the paper.' With this warning, Koroku started to take up the panels, beginning with the veranda of the *chanoma*.

To the right of Koroku was his own room, which went off at an angle from the veranda. To his left was the front entrance, jutting out from the rest of the house. In front of him a hedge ran parallel to the veranda. Thus a square enclosure was formed, which in summer was filled with cosmos. Sosuke and Oyone enjoyed looking out each morning at the dew-covered blossoms. Just in front of the hedge they had set up bamboo sticks and planted morning glories to twine about them. As soon as they got up in the morning, they would hurry to the veranda and count with pleasure the number of blossoms that were in bloom that day. But from autumn to the end of winter the grass and the flowers were dried out and lifeless, and the little garden looked more like an untended plot than a flower bed. In this season it moved them to sad melancholy rather than to joy. With this frost-covered square plot of garden behind him, Koroku worked away, tearing the old paper from the *shoji*.

Occasionally a cold blast of wind attacked him from the back, especially about his neck and shaven head. Each blast made him want to retreat from the exposure of the veranda to the warmth of his own room. Moving his hands, red with the cold and wind, without speaking, he wrung out his rag in a bucket and continued to rub down the frame of the *shoji*.

'You must be very cold. I'm sorry. Unfortunately, the weather's turned bad.' Oyone's words were kind, as she poured hot water from the tea-kettle to dilute the paste she had prepared the day before.

Inwardly Koroku deeply resented being asked to do this kind of work. As he rubbed down the frame, he was filled with the feeling that it was something of an insult to ask it of him, especially in view of the circumstances in which he had unavoidably been placed. He recalled that when in the past he had had to help out by doing the same chore at his uncle's house, he had considered it a good way of passing the time, and far from finding it unpleasant, actually enjoyed it. But now it seemed to him that he was being looked down upon as having no better talent than for this kind of menial work. The cold of the veranda served to intensify his resentment.

In this mood his responses to Oyone's words of solicitude were very curt. A law student who had lived in the same lodging with him, he recalled, used to stop on the way home from a walk and casually spend as much as five yen on toilet articles. There was no reason, he felt, why he alone should fall into such penury. The lot of his brother and sister, who were content to spend their entire lives in such circumstances, seemed to him pitiable indeed. They worried about spending even the little additional money it would have taken to buy good paper to cover the *shoji*. In Koroku's eyes this could hardly be called living.

'With this paper, these will have to be redone again in no time.' Koroku unrolled a length of paper, held it up to the sun, and slapped it two or three times, full strength, with the back of his hand.

'Do you think so? But since we don't have any children,

they should last for quite a while.' Oyone dabbed paste on the frame with her brush. The two took hold of the long strip of paper, one on each side, and tried to stretch it so that there would be no slack. Occasionally Koroku's face would reflect the impatience he felt, and Oyone, seeing it, would feel constraint and cut the paper with her razor blade before it was properly stretched out. As a result, a number of very conspicuous wrinkles remained even after they had finished. Standing up the completed panels and inspecting them, Oyone was displeased, and in her heart she wished that it were her husband helping her instead of Koroku.

'There are a few wrinkles, aren't there?'

'I'm very awkward at this sort of thing.'

'Nonsense. Your brother isn't any better. Besides, he's always a great deal more abstracted than you are.'

Koroku made no answer. He took the bowl which Kiyo brought from the kitchen and placed it in front of the re-papered *shoji*. Then he sprayed the *shoji* until the paper was wet all over. By the time he had finished the second *shoji*, the first was already dry, and the wrinkles had almost disappeared. When he started on the third *shoji*, Koroku complained that his back ached. Oyone herself had had a headache since morning.

'Let's do one more, and the *shoji* for the *chanoma* will be finished. Then we can rest,' she said.

When they had finished the *shoji* of the *chanoma*, it was already noon, and so they sat down to lunch. Since Koroku had moved in several days before, Oyone, in Sosuke's absence, sat opposite him at lunch. Until now, she had never eaten alone with anyone but Sosuke. For many years it had been her custom to take her meals by herself when he was away. It was quite an unwonted experience to suddenly find herself sitting across the table from this brother-in-law, taking her lunch face to face with him. All was well as long as Kiyo was at work in the kitchen, but when Kiyo could no longer be seen or heard, she felt extremely ill at ease. Of course, she was older than Koroku, and, moreover, the very nature of their relationship until now was not such as could easily generate the kind of romantic atmosphere that is apt to develop between two people of the opposite sex placed in such a situation. Oyone wondered when this feeling of constraint at dining alone with Koroku would disappear. Before he had moved in with them, she had not foreseen this problem, and so she was all the more confused. Since there was nothing to be done about it, she did her best to carry on a conversation with him as they ate, or at least to fill in embarrassing pauses. Unfortunately, Koroku at this point could not find in himself either the composure or the discernment to set his sister-in-law at ease.

'Koroku, did you have good food at your lodging?'

Koroku could not give a simple, unaffected answer to such a question as he used to be able to when he came to visit them from his lodging. Since he had to make some reply, he muttered only, 'No, not very good.' But there was a tone of insincerity in his voice, and Oyone wondered if he reproached her for not treating him well enough. Then this feeling in turn, though it remained unspoken, transmitted itself to Koroku.

Today, especially, because of her headache, she could not bring herself to make the usual effort at conversation as she sat with him at table. To attempt it and fail would be all the more disagreeable. Thus the two finished their meal in even greater silence than when they were working together on the *shoji*.

In the afternoon the work went more smoothly than in the morning, perhaps because they were now more accustomed to it. On the other hand, the constraint they felt towards each other grew rather than lessened. The cold was partly responsible. When they got up from table, the clouds had dispersed. It was now so clear that the sky, with the sun in the centre, seemed to be moving away from them. But then, once again, clouds suddenly appeared to drive away the blue. As it grew darker and darker, the eye of the sun was sealed, and it looked as if it might snow. The two took turns warming their hands over the brazier.

'My brother gets a rise next month, doesn't he?' Koroku suddenly asked Oyone, who had just picked up a scrap of paper from the floor and was wiping her hands.

'Why is that?' She obviously knew nothing about it.

'But didn't you read in the newspaper that government employees would be getting a rise next year?'

Oyone didn't know anything about it. She asked Koroku to explain the details. When he had finished, she nodded in approval.

'It's about time. With his present salary no one could make ends meet. Everything has gone up so. The price of fish, for example, has already doubled in the short time we've been in Tokyo.'

This time it was Koroku's turn to manifest ignorance. He hadn't realized that the price of fish had risen so abruptly.

Since Koroku showed some interest in the subject, their conversation flowed along more smoothly than usual. Oyone repeated to him what Sosuke had told her of his conversation with Sakai the day he had taken up the letter-box . . . that when Sakai was about eighteen or nineteen, prices were extremely low. Buckwheat noodles cost from eight rin to two sen five rin. One portion of beef could be had for four sen. Even sirloin cost only six. You could be entertained at a *yose* for three or four. If a student received seven yen a month from home, he could get along, and if he got ten, he was thought to be well-off.

'You wouldn't have had any trouble getting through college in those days, would you?'

'And my brother would have found it much easier to make a comfortable living.'

It was already past three when they finished the *shoji*

of the parlour. Sosuke would be back soon, and Oyone had to begin preparations for dinner. So they decided to call it a day and began to put things back. Koroku stretched himself and hit his head with clenched fists several times.

'Thank you for your help. You must be tired.'

Koroku remembered the box of cakes Sakai had brought to Sosuke in token of gratitude for the return of the letter-box. He asked Oyone to bring it out, and they had tea and cake together.

'Is Sakai a college graduate?'

'Yes, they say he is.'

Koroku smoked and drank his tea. Finally he asked again, 'Then my brother said nothing at all to you about the coming salary rise?'

'No, not a word,' replied Oyone.

'It would be nice to be like him — no complaints about anything. . . .'

Oyone made no answer to this, and Koroku rose and went off to his own room. After a time he came back, carrying his brazier, saying that the fire had gone out.

Though he was now in his brother's care, Koroku still believed his cousin, Yasunosuke, when he encouraged him, saying that before too long he would be able to do something for him. In the light of this promise he did not withdraw completely from school but applied instead for a temporary leave of absence.

IX

As a result of the letter-box incident Sosuke and his landlord struck up an unexpected acquaintanceship. Until that time their only contact had consisted in Sosuke's commissioning Kiyo once a month to go up to pay the rent, and Sakai's handing her a receipt in exchange. Sosuke had no more feeling of neighbourliness toward the man at the top of the hill than if that man had been a foreigner.

On the afternoon of the day on which Sosuke had returned the letter-box, a detective came, just as Sakai had foreseen, to look over the place where the box had been found. Sakai accompanied him, so that Oyone was able to catch her first glimpse of the man she had heard so much about. Two things were somewhat unexpected: first, that he did have a beard, though she had heard he didn't; and secondly, that he should use such polite language even to her.

'He does have a beard after all,' she exclaimed to Sosuke when he had come back from work that afternoon.

Two days later Sakai's maid brought over a handsome box of cakes with Sakai's card. She conveyed her master's thanks, as well as his apology for not coming over himself.

That evening Sosuke opened the box, and as he stuffed one of the cakes into his mouth, he said, 'He can't be so stingy after all, if he sends over such a nice gift. That story about not letting the neighbours' kids use his swings can't be true.'

'I'm sure it isn't.' Oyone also defended Sakai.

But although they had become so much more intimate with Sakai than before the thief had made his appearance, it never occurred to either Sosuke or Oyone to try to increase this intimacy. To turn this new-found familiarity to their own ends was, of course, far from their thoughts. The couple lacked the courage to take any step forward to greater intimacy, even with the motive of friendliness towards a neighbour. If events had been allowed to take their natural course, their relationship would have reverted before long to the old impersonal one of landlord and tenant. The distance between their hearts would have continued to be symbolized by the cliff that separated their houses, as it had before.

But on the third day after the theft, just as it was getting dark, Sakai suddenly appeared at their door, wearing a heavy mantle with an otter-fur collar. The couple, unaccustomed to having evening visitors, were surprised to the point of consternation. They showed him into the parlour, and he thanked Sosuke politely for his help three days before.

'Thanks to you, I was able to recover the stolen articles.' Then he detached from the gold watch-chain wound about his waist-sash a double-cased gold watch and showed it to them.

He had reported the theft to the police, since there was a regulation requiring him to do so, but it was a very old watch and he did not consider it much of a loss. Of course he hadn't expected to get it back. Then suddenly, the day before, a small package without the sender's address arrived, and in it he found his watch.

'The thief must have used it for a time. Or perhaps he tried to sell it and finding it would fetch very little, decided to return it to its owner. In any case, this is a rare occurrence.' Sakai laughed, and continued, 'But to tell the truth, it is the letter-box that is of value to me. It was given to my grandmother when she was in service at the palace long ago. It's a kind of family heirloom.'

That evening Sakai spent about two hours chatting with them. Both Sosuke, sitting talking with him, and Oyone, listening from the *chanoma,* couldn't help marvelling at the breadth of his conversation. After he had gone, Oyone remarked,

'His world is very large, isn't it?'

'It should be, with all the time he has on his hands,' Sosuke replied.

The next day, on his way home from work, Sosuke had just got off the streetcar and was standing in front of the shop that had bought the Hoitsu screen, when he caught sight of Sakai's mantle with the otter-fur collar. He was speaking to the owner of the shop, facing away from the street. The owner was looking up at him from behind his huge horn-rimmed glasses. Sosuke didn't think it necessary to stop to greet him, and tried to pass by without doing so. But just as he reached the front of the store, Sakai happened to look towards the street.

'Many thanks for last night. Are you returning from work?' Sakai addressed him in a very easy and cheerful manner. Sosuke couldn't just walk past without speaking to him. Slackening his pace, he tipped his hat. Sakai, seeming to have finished his business, came out of the shop.

'Are you looking for something?' asked Sosuke.

'Nothing in particular,' answered Sakai, and he walked along with Sosuke in the direction of their homes.

When they had walked a short distance, Sakai remarked, 'That old man, he's really sly. He brought over a fake Kazan the other day and tried to pass it off as real. I've just been giving him a piece of my mind.'

It occurred to Sosuke for the first time that Sakai, like many men of means, undoubtedly made a hobby of collecting *objets d'art*. How much better to have shown the Hoitsu screen, which he had sold the other day, to a man like Sakai.

'Does he know a lot about *kakemono*?'

'Quite the contrary. In fact, he doesn't know a thing. One look at his shop will tell you that. He doesn't have anything even remotely resembling an antique or *objet d'art* there. He started out collecting scrap paper and built up the shop to what it is now.'

Sakai was well acquanted with the history of the shopkeeper. According to the old man who made the deliveries for the local grocer, Sakai's house had been a very important one in feudal days. It was the oldest family of good lineage in the area. Sosuke recalled vaguely having heard that at the time of the fall of the *bakufu* the family had taken refuge in Shizuoka, or else that it had gone and come back again, but he had no clear recollection of exactly what it was he had heard.

'When he was a boy, he was always playing tricks on others. He was the bully of the neighbourhood and often got into fights,' said Sakai, referring to the days when they were boys together. When Sosuke asked why he had schemed to have him buy a fake Kazan, Sakai laughed and gave the following explanation.

'We've been buying from him since my father's time. Occasionally he will drop in with some trifle or other. But he has little taste and a great deal of greed. He's tough to deal with. Then the other day he got me to buy a Hoitsu screen from him, and so he was encouraged by this success to try something else.'

Sosuke was stunned. But he couldn't very well break into Sakai's stream of explanation, so he remained quiet. According to Sakai, the man, inflated with his success, had been bringing him all kinds of *kakemono*, of which he himself had very little understanding. He had a piece of what he called *Korai* china, which had in fact been baked in Osaka. But thinking it the genuine article, he displayed it prominently in his shop.

At the end Sakai concluded, 'The only thing you can safely buy from him is a kitchen table or a new tea-kettle.'

They had reached the top of the slope. From here Sakai had to turn right, and Sosuke, to go down the hill. Sosuke would have liked to accompany him a bit further and ask for more details about the screen, but it would seem strange to make such a detour, he reflected, and so they parted. Before going their separate ways, Sosuke asked Sakai,

'Would it be all right for me to call on you one of these days?'

'By all means. Please do,' Sakai answered with good grace.

That day there was no wind and the sun even emerged briefly. But inside the house Oyone felt a chill that pene-

94

trated to the bone. She set up a makeshift *kotatsu*, using Sosuke's kimono as a covering, and placed it in the middle of the parlour. There she sat waiting for her husband to come home from work.

It was the first time this winter that she had set up a *kotatsu* during the day. At night, of course, they had been using one for a long time, but they had always put it in the room now occupied by Koroku.

'Why do you place that thing here in the middle of the parlour?'

'But it's not likely that anyone will call. Isn't it all right? Now that Koroku's in the next room we can't put it there any more.'

Sosuke had forgoten about Koroku's moving in. He put on a warm kimono, without removing his shirt, and wound the sash about him several times and tied it.

'This is the cold side of the house. Without a *kotatsu* the cold is more than I can bear.' The mats in Koroku's room were old and soiled, but since there were windows facing east and south, it was the warmest room in the house.

Sosuke took a couple of sips of the warm tea Oyone brought him, and asked, 'Is Koroku in?' Koroku was almost certainly in his room, but the room was absolutely still, as if it were empty. Oyone rose to call him, but Sosuke stopped her, saying he had no particular business with him. Then he crawled into the *kotatsu* himself and stretched out on his side. The shades of evening were already beginning to fall in the room, cut off as it was on one side by the overhanging cliff. Sosuke lay, head pillowed on his hand, thinking of nothing in particular, just staring out into the bleak, gradually darkening corridor that separated the house from the cliff. In this mood the sounds of Oyone and Kiyo at work in the kitchen were as unrelated to him as if they came from next door. Finally the room became so dark that all that could be made out was the white of the *shoji*. Still he did not move from the *kotatsu* or call for a lamp.

When he emerged from the dark to take his place at table for the evening meal, Koroku came out of his room and sat opposite him. Oyone joined them, but remembered that she had forgotten to put the *amado* of the parlour in place, and rose to do so at once. Sosuke would have liked to tell Koroku that in the evenings he ought to help his sister-in-law prepare the lamp and put out the *amado*. But since Koroku had just arrived, he thought it best to avoid possible unpleasantness for the present. So he said nothing.

The two brothers waited until Oyone returned to the room before taking up their chopsticks. Sosuke chose that moment to tell Oyone that he had met Sakai on his way home in front of the second-hand shop, and that Sakai had told him that he had bought a Hoitsu screen there from the man with the huge glasses.

Oyone said only, 'He did?' and looked for a time at her husband.

'It must be the same screen. I'm sure of it.'

Koroku did not enter into the conversation at first, but as he listened to them, he gradually began to understand what they were talking about.

'How much did you get for the screen?' he asked. Before answering, Oyone looked at her husband.

At the end of the meal Koroku returned at once to his room, and Sosuke to the *kotatsu*. After a time Oyone too came to warm herself in the *kotatsu*. They decided it might be good if Sosuke called on Sakai the following Saturday or Sunday and had a look at the screen.

When Sunday arrived, Sosuke once again indulged himself in the pleasurable late sleep that could be his only once a week, so that when he finally rose, there was almost nothing left of the morning. Oyone was complaining of a headache and sat braced against the brazier, completely inert. Seeing her, Sosuke reflected that if the little room were still unoccupied, she would have been able to spend the day there in bed. In giving up the room to Koroku, he had indirectly deprived her of her place of refuge, and he felt sorry for her.

He urged her to lay out the bedding in the parlour and go back to bed if she were not feeling well. But Oyone was reluctant to do this. At least she might set up the *kotatsu* and he would also make use of it. Finally Oyone had Kiyo bring in what was needed for the *kotatsu* and she made it ready.

Koroku had left the house shortly before Sosuke got up, so that he had not even caught a glimpse of him that day. Sosuke did not try to find out from Oyone where he had gone. Recently he had been trying to spare Oyone the embarrassment of having to answer his questions about Koroku and his activities. He even thought at times that the situation would be less painful if she were openly critical of his brother.

Even at noon Oyone did not come out from the *kotatsu*. Sosuke, thinking it best that she get as much quiet sleep as possible, stole silently into the kitchen and informed Kiyo that he was going to call on Sakai at the top of the hill. He put on a short coat over his kimono and left the house.

Emerging from the dark room into the front street, his depression suddenly lifted. He felt pleasure in the resistance his skin and muscles put up to the chilling wind and in the sudden expansion of his spirits as they came out of their winter cramps. It wasn't good for Oyone to spend all her time indoors. When the weather turned fine, he would have to get her to go out and breathe fresh air, he reflected as he walked along.

When he passed through the gate to Sakai's, he saw something red and foreign to winter in the hedge separating the front entrance from the back. Approaching for a closer look, he saw that it was a doll's nightgown. One sleeve had been passed through a thin bamboo stick, which had then been propped into the branches of the hawthorn so as not to fall. He admired the resourcefulness of the little girl who had done this. To Sosuke, who had no experience of bringing up children, much less of a girl of an age to play house, the quite ordinary sight of the doll's red kimono hanging out in the sun had great charm, and he stood looking at it for a time. He recalled how some twenty years ago on Girls' Day his parents used to set out the traditional display of dolls for his little sister, now long dead. Displayed with the dolls had been an assortment of cakes of beautiful patterns, and white sake which looked sweet but was actually quite bitter.

Sakai was at home but he was in the middle of his lunch. Sosuke was asked to wait for a few minutes. No sooner had he settled himself on the cushion offered him than he heard voices in the next room, which he surmised to be those of the children who had hung the tiny doll's dress out in the hawthorn bush. When the maid, bringing him tea, opened the sliding panels that separated the two rooms, he caught sight of four large eyes peering at him from the shadows of the room. The maid then brought him a brazier to warm himself, and this time as she left the room he detected still another face. Perhaps because it was his first real visit here, it seemed to him that each time the panels opened a different face was looking out at him, and he wondered how many children there actually were. When at length the maid left him to himself, one of the children opened the panels just a crack, and a sparkling black eye stared out at him. Sosuke was intrigued and made a silent gesture of invitation. At this the panels slammed shut and three or four voices could be heard laughing on the other side.

Then after a time he heard one of the girls say, 'Let's play "house" again today.'

Another girl, who might have been the older sister of the first, replied, 'Fine. But today let's play it Western style. Tosaku, since you're the father, we'll call you "papa". And

Yukiko, you're the mother, so we'll call you "mama". Do you understand?'

Still another voice popped in. 'It sounds funny to be called "mama".' And she laughed gleefully.

'I'm always the grandmother. There must be a Western name for her too, isn't there?'

'I suppose "grandmama" will do,' the older sister suggested.

Then for some time the children could be heard exchanging greetings, mixed with simulated telephone conversations. It all sounded very strange but pleasant to Sosuke.

He heard footsteps approaching. Before joining him, Sakai stepped into the next room and cautioned the children, 'This is no place to be making a lot of noise. We have a guest. Go and play somewhere else.'

'I don't want to. I won't go unless you promise to buy me a big pony,' one of the children answered back at once. He sounded very young and had trouble forming his words, so that it took him some time to get out his plea. Sosuke found this very charming too.

By the time his host had joined him and apologized for having kept him waiting, the children had gone off to play elsewhere.

'It's wonderfully lively here.' Sosuke was only putting his feelings into words, but Sakai seemed to take the remark as social convention.

'You can see how disorderly they are,' said Sakai, half-apologetically, and he went on to give Sosuke a number of examples of what he had to put up with. Once they had filled a beautiful Chinese flower basket with charcoal balls and put it in the *tokonoma* in place of the regular flower arrangement. On another occasion they had filled his boots with water and dumped the goldfish into them. This all had a fresh and appealing sound to Sosuke. Sakai went on to say that with so many girls someone was always in need of new clothes. And they were growing so fast that when they took a trip for a couple of weeks, he inevitably discovered on their return that they had shot up another inch. He felt as if he were being pursued. Before he knew it, it would be time to get them ready for marriage, and then he expected to wind up in the poorhouse. Childless Sosuke was unable to summon up much sympathy for the plight of his host. On the contrary, the more Sakai complained about his children, the more envious Sosuke felt of this man whose general attitude and appearance belied the truth of what he was saying.

Sosuke waited for just the right moment and then asked if Sakai would show him the screen he had spoken about the other day. The latter agreed at once, and, clapping his hands, called a servant. He told him to bring the screen out of the store-room, where it had been put away. Looking at Sosuke, he said,

'It was standing over there until just two or three days ago, but the children were always gathering behind it and playing all kinds of games there. I was afraid they might injure it. So I put it away.'

Hearing Sakai's explanation, Sosuke was sorry for having put him to so much trouble and felt uncomfortable about it. To tell the truth, his curiosity about the screen was really not that strong. Whether an object in another's possession had once been his or not, nothing was really to be gained by ascertaining the fact.

Nevertheless, the screen, as Sosuke had requested, was brought out to the veranda and placed before him. Just as he had expected, it was the very screen that until the other day had stood in his own parlour. In discovering the fact, Sosuke experienced no particular emotion. But looking at the screen now in the setting in which he sat — the fresh *tatami*, the nicely-grained wood of the ceiling, the good taste of the *tokonoma*, the beautifully-patterned sliding doors connecting to the next room — and seeing how carefully the two servants had handled it in bringing it out of the store-room, it now seemed at least ten times as valuable as when he had possessed it. Since the right words did not come immediately to his lips, he just continued to look at this object with which he was already so familiar.

Sakai mistakenly took Sosuke for a connoisseur. He stood with his hand resting on the edge of the screen, looking alternately at Sosuke's face and at the screen. Since Sosuke made no comment, he himself broke the silence.

'This is a genuine piece. Quality will out.'

Sosuke answered only, 'Yes.'

Finally Sakai walked round behind Sosuke and pointed out several features of the screen, praising and explaining. The painter, great artist that he was, had been prodigal in his use of paint, he commented. This was his special characteristic. The colour, therefore, was superb. All this was new to Sosuke, though much of what Sakai said was common knowledge to anyone in the field.

After a decent interval had elapsed, Sosuke offered his thanks and returned to where he had been sitting. His host also returned to his place and began to speak of many things, especially of epitaphs and scrolls. Sakai seemed to be very interested in calligraphy and in *haiku*. He was knowledgeable in so many fields that Sosuke wondered when he had found the time to cram so much learning into his head. Sosuke was embarrassed at his own ignorance and tried to speak as little as possible and just listen to the words of his companion.

Sakai saw that Sosuke had little interest in scrolls and turned the conversation to the subject of painting. He offered to show Sosuke his collection, though — he added modestly — it didn't amount to much. Despite the good will with which the offer was made, Sosuke could only refuse. Instead, apologizing beforehand for the bluntness of his question, he asked Sakai how much he had paid for the Hoitsu screen.

'It was a real find. I was able to buy it for eighty yen,' he answered immediately.

Sosuke wondered if he should tell Sakai about the screen or not, and thinking that a full confession of the matter might be interesting to him, he plunged into his explanation, leaving out none of the details. Sakai listened in silence, punctuated by an occasional exclamation. At the end he said,

'Then you didn't come to see the screen because you were interested in painting, did you?' And he burst out laughing at his mistake, as if this too had been an interesting experience. But at the same time he expressed regret that he had not bought the screen directly from Sosuke for something nearer its true value. It was really too bad. He launched into a diatribe against the 'antique' dealer who had sold it to him.

After this meeting Sosuke and Sakai became very intimate.

X

Neither Mrs Saeki nor her son, Yasunosuke, had been to call on Sosuke for a long time. Sosuke, for his part, had neither the leisure nor the inclination to visit them. Though they were his relatives, they might as well have lived under a different sun.

Koroku occasionally saw them, but his visits too, it seemed, were very infrequent, and on his return he seldom gave Oyone news of what was happening in the Saeki family. Oyone even wondered at times if he did not purposely refrain from speaking to her about them as a way of getting back at her. But since she had nothing either to gain or to lose from maintaining good relations with the Saekis, she was more pleased than otherwise at not having to listen to Koroku's account of them. Their name sometimes came up, however, when the brothers were talking together. About a week earlier she had overheard Koroku telling Sosuke that Yasunosuke was at present hard at work trying to patent another new invention, this time a printing press that printed clearly without using ink. From the little she overheard, she gathered that the machine must be a very valuable one. But since the discussion was above her head and of its very nature unconnected — either for good or for bad — with herself, she kept her usual silence and did not enter into the conversation. Sosuke, being a man, had considerable curiosity as to how the machine worked. He asked how it was possible to print without using ink, and other questions.

Koroku, who was not a specialist in the field, could not be expected to give a detailed answer. He merely repeated what he remembered of Yasu's explanation. It was a printing process that had recently been invented in Great Britain. Basically it was only another applied use of electricity. One pole was attached to the type and another to the paper. To print, it was only necessary to run the paper over the type. The print was usually black, but it was very easy to adjust the machine to print in red or blue, so that the time usually required for the ink to dry before applying another colour could now be saved. Yasunosuke had pointed out that it was a most promising enterprise, since in printing a newspaper, for example, the new process saved the cost of ink and ink rollers and cut down the work involved by about a quarter. Yasu had spoken as if the rosy future he predicted for this machine were already a fact, and his eyes had sparkled as if he beheld his own future prosperity in that of the machine. Sosuke listened silently to Koroku's account, and when he had heard him out, he still made no comment. To tell the truth, he was sceptical about the invention. It might work, and then again it might not. One would have to wait to find out before passing judgment.

'Then he's given up on fishing boats?' asked Oyone, who had been silent until now.

'He hasn't given up exactly, but it seems that a good bit of capital is needed to fit out a fishing boat with a motor. Despite its convenience, not every owner can afford one.' Koroku sounded rather as if he were defending Yasunosuke. The three continued the conversation for some time and ended on the following note.

'After all, every project has its hitches,' said Sosuke.

'The best off is Mr Sakai,' concluded Oyone. 'With all his money he's able to take life easy.'

Then Koroku returned to his room.

In this way news of the Saekis occasionally reached the ears of Sosuke and Oyone, but they went for long periods without knowing how they were getting on.

One day Oyone asked Sosuke, 'Does Koroku receive money from Yasu when he visits him?'

Sosuke, who had not paid very close attention to his brother's comings and goings, asked immediately, 'Why do you ask?'

'He's been drinking quite a bit of sake lately.'

'I suppose Yasu plies him with sake as a fee for listening to his bluster about all the money he's making on these new inventions.' And Sosuke laughed. The conversation did not go further.

Three days after that, Koroku failed to return home in time for dinner. They waited a while, but Sosuke complained he was hungry. He ignored Oyone's suggestion that he go over to the bath before dinner, and he began to eat.

It was then that Oyone asked, 'Couldn't you persuade Koroku to stop drinking?'

'Is he drinking enough to have to speak to him about it?' Sosuke made a wry face.

Oyone admitted that he was probably not drinking that much, but that she was worried to see him come home with such a red face in the daytime when no one else was around. Sosuke made no further remark but wondered secretly if Oyone could be right. Was Koroku borrowing money somewhere just to buy sake, which he was not particularly fond of in the first place?

The end of the year was approaching. Night now had firm hold on two-thirds of the day. Almost every day the wind blew. The sound of it alone was enough to cast a dark cloud over life. Koroku remained shut up in his room and found each day almost more than he could bear. The more he tried to think calmly, the more his head began to spin and the harder he found it to remain in his room. But it was still more unpleasant to go out to the *chanoma* and have to exchange words with his sister-in-law. He chose instead to leave the house. He made the rounds of his friends. At first these friends treated him as they always had, and joined with him in the lively conversation characteristic of young students. But after they had exhausted all topics of conversation and he still kept coming, they judged that he came solely out of boredom, and they grew tired of listening to the same things over and over again. Sometimes when he called, they made it clear that they were busy with class preparations. He found it very unpleasant to be ignored by them and to be treated as if he were merely lazy or without ambition. But at home he lacked the peace of mind either for reading or for thinking. In short, the turmoil he experienced within and the restrictions imposed from without conspired to inhibit him from making the efforts and acquiring the virtues necessary to achieve a maturity corresponding to his years.

There were days when it was too much trouble to leave the house, as when a cold wind-driven rain made it impossible to go out without getting soaked, or when, as a result of the melting snow, the mud on the streets rose — or splashed — above the *geta* to wet and soil the white *tabi*. Koroku would stay at home on these days, but he didn't seem to know what to do with himself. He would come out of his room occasionally, sit beside the brazier, and pour himself a cup of tea. If Oyone happened to be there, he might even make small talk with her for a while.

'Do you like sake?' Oyone had once asked him.

On another occasion she said, 'It will be New Year soon. How much *zoni* can you eat?'

As these occasions to converse grew in frequency the two gradually came to be on better terms. Koroku did not even hesitate to ask Oyone to do little things for him, such as mending the tear in his coat. As she mended his coat-sleeve, he just sat there motionless, watching her fingers at work. When it was her husband who sat before her like this, she worked away in silence, feeling no need to talk. With Koroku, she could not be so casual. Instead she made a laboured effort to keep a conversation going. The subject that came most naturally to Koroku's lips was that of concern for his future.

'But you're still very young. You have your whole life still before you. You mustn't give up hope. Your brother will find something for you.' She had tried to console him a couple of times in this fashion. The third time the subject came up, she added, 'Besides, hasn't Yasunosuke promised to help you next year?'

Koroku's face wore an expression of uncertainty as he answered, 'If Yasu does as he promised, everything'll be all right. But I'm not sure how far I can trust in his promises, especially since the fishing boat project doesn't seem to be making much profit.'

Seeing this depressed Koroku sitting there in front of her and comparing him to the Koroku who sometimes came home at night reeking of sake, and who always seemed to be worked up and angry about something, and so full of resentment, Oyone felt both pity and amusement.

'Really, if your brother only had a little money, he'd do whatever he could for you.' Her words were from the heart and full of a warm sympathy.

It may have been that same evening. Koroku again wrapped his heavy mantle about him and ventured out into the cold. A little after eight o'clock he returned, carrying a long, narrow white bag, which he placed before Oyone, saying, 'It's very cold tonight, so I thought we might have some *soba* before going to bed. I bought this on my way back from the Saekis.' And while Oyone boiled some water, he cut up slices of dried bonito to give the *soba* flavour.

Koroku told the couple the latest news from the Saekis: that Yasu's wedding had been postponed until spring. The first steps towards the match had been taken shortly after Yasu's graduation from college, and arrangements were already nearing completion when Koroku returned from Boshu and was informed by his aunt that she was no longer able to assume responsibility for his school expenses. Since no formal announcement had come, Sosuke and Oyone did not know what date had finally been agreed upon, but from the fragments of news brought them by Koroku from his occasional visits to the Saekis, they expected it to take place within the year. From Koroku too they learned that the bride's father was a company employee, that the family was quite comfortably off, that she was a graduate of a girls' academy and had many brothers and sisters. Only Koroku had seen her picture.

'Is she pretty?' Oyone had asked.

'I suppose you might say so,' Koroku had answered.

The subject of their conversation that evening, as they sat down to eat the *soba*, was the reason for postponing the marriage. Oyone surmised that they had found it to be an unlucky time, but Sosuke thought it was because they didn't have long enough to make the necessary preparations.

Koroku disagreed with both. 'I think the reason is financial. The bride's family seems to be the kind that likes to do things in style. Auntie's got to follow suit.' It was not usual for Koroku to think in such practical terms.

107

XI

It was in late autumn, when the fiery red maple leaves had begun to wither and turn brown, that Oyone's health took a turn for the worse. Apart from the days in Kyoto, she had never enjoyed very good health, either in Hiroshima or in Fukuoka, and even after returning to Tokyo she could not be said to be really well. The more she thought about it, the more irresistible was the conclusion that the air of her native Tokyo was especially uncongenial to her. Still, she had seemed slightly better lately and had given Sosuke only occasional cause for alarm about her condition, so that he was able to do his work at the office without worrying about how she was faring in his absence. The wind of late autumn, breaking the icicles as it swept by, became bitingly cold. Oyone felt somewhat indisposed, but not to the extent of saying anything about it to Sosuke. She was afraid that he would want her to see a doctor, which would place an additional burden on their already straitened finances.

It was then that Koroku moved in with them. Sosuke, knowing the delicate balance of Oyone's health — both physical and mental — as only a husband could know it, had not wanted to further complicate matters by introducing another member to the household. But in the face of circumstances he had no other choice but to take Koroku in and let events run their natural course. He realized the contradiction in his words when he advised his wife to take things as easy as possible.

Oyone only smiled and answered, 'It's all right. You needn't worry about me.' Her reply had the effect of making him worry all the more. Strangely enough, however, she began to feel much better after Koroku had moved in. She seemed to take new life as a result of her new responsibilities, and she was more energetic than ever in the care of her husband and of her newly-arrived brother-in-law. This was all lost on Koroku, but Sosuke realized only too well how much more effort she was expending now than before. At the same time as he felt new gratitude for her devotion, he feared that, as a result of this additional strain, her health, which had never been good, might collapse altogether.

His fears, unfortunately, were suddenly realized towards the end of December. He was thrown into confusion as if the powder of his premonitions had finally been ignited. It was a bitter cold day, and layer upon layer of cloud concealed the sky. Oyone, who had been unable to sleep the night before, felt the results of the lack of rest, but she summoned up strength to begin the daily round. As she went about her work, she felt a certain amount of pain in her chest, but rather than go back to bed, where only her mind would be active, she preferred to let the stimulus of external activity give her a measure of relief, and help her get through the day. Until she had seen her husband off to work, at any rate, she put up with the pain, expecting that it would go away after a time as it always did. But once Sosuke had left the house and the first round of the day's tasks had been accomplished, her taut nerves relaxed and the gloomy weather began to depress her. The sky looked as if it were frozen, and cold seemed to be seeping into the room through the paper of the darkened *shoji*. Despite the cold, her forehead started to burn with fever. There was nothing for her to do but spread out once again on the parlour *tatami* the bedding she had earlier put away, and lie down. When even this did not give relief, she had Kiyo wring out a wet towel and place it on her forehead. But the towel lost its chill in no time, and she had Kiyo place a basin of iced water beside her pillow so that she could change towels every few minutes.

Until noon she kept on cooling her forehead in this primitive fashion, but the fever gave no sign of abating. She lacked the strength to get up, even to take the midday meal with Koroku. Instead she told Kiyo to make his lunch and take it to him in his room, while she herself remained in bed. She exchanged her own hard pillow for the soft, stuffed pillow of her husband. She no longer had enough spirit to care if her hair-do came undone.

Koroku came out of his room, opened the sliding door to the parlour a crack, and looked in. Oyone was half facing the *tokonoma* with eyes closed. Thinking that perhaps she was asleep, he didn't say a word but quietly slid the doors back into place. Then, sitting alone in front of the large table they used for their meals, he bolted his rice gruel, making sucking noises all the while.

About two o'clock Oyone finally dozed off. When she awoke, the wet towel on her forehead had become so warm that it was almost dry. Her head felt a bit better, but now a new oppressiveness took hold of her from the neck to the base of the spine. All the same, thinking it would be worse if she didn't take a little nourishment, she rose and had a very light lunch.

'How are you feeling?' asked Kiyo, deeply concerned, as she waited on Oyone. Since she seemed to be much better, she asked Kiyo to put away the bedding, and she placed herself beside the brazier to await Sosuke's return from work.

Sosuke arrived home on the dot. He told her that the banners advertising end-of-year sales were already to be seen in the streets of Kanda and that the sales had already begun. A red and white curtain was hanging in the emporium and a band playing away to spur on sales.

'The place is full of life. You ought to go and see for yourself. It's just a short ride on the streetcar.' he urged. His face was red, as if it had been bitten by the cold.

Listening to Sosuke's words, full of solicitude, Oyone couldn't bring herself to tell him she was ill. The fact was that she no longer felt so bad. So she put on her usual face. As if nothing were wrong, she helped him to change his clothes, then folded his suit away carefully. By this time it was evening.

About nine o'clock she turned suddenly to Sosuke and told him she was feeling a little under the weather and would like to go to bed early. Since she had seemed until then to be in good spirits and had carried on a conversation with him in her usual manner, Sosuke was somewhat taken aback. But reassured by her that it was nothing serious, he put aside his anxiety and bade her get ready for bed.

After she had retired, he sat up for another twenty minutes or so, listening to the song of the tea-kettle on the brazier, his lamp lighting the quiet night. He thought of the rumour he had heard that employees of public offices would receive a rise in salary next year. He had also heard that in all probability there would first be a reorganization of the offices and a weeding-out of employees. In that case, he wondered, in which category would he find himself — necessary or redundant? He regretted that Sugihara, the friend who had called him to Tokyo, was no longer a section head in his office. Since coming to Tokyo, strange to say, he had never once been ill, which meant that he had not missed even a single day at work. Inasmuch as he had not finished university and did almost no reading, his learning was below average. But his mind was not so bad that he was not up to the work assigned him. Considering the matter from many different angles, he decided that he would probably survive the purge, and he tapped the tea-kettle lightly with his fingernails.

Suddenly from the parlour he heard Oyone call out in pain, 'Sosuke, Sosuke!' Forgetting himself, he rose and rushed to her side. Her eyebrows were contracted in agony, and her right hand was pressing down on her shoulder. She was half out of the covers. Almost as a reflex action, he brought his hand to her shoulder and took a firm grip of the bone immediately above the place where she was pressing.

111

'A little farther to the back,' she pleaded. It took two or three tries to find the right place. When he found it, he probed with his finger and felt a lump as hard as a rock in a hollow a little towards the back from where her neck and shoulder were joined. She begged him to press down on it as hard as he could. Sweat broke out on his forehead, but still he could not press hard enough to suit her.

He remembered that the old people used to call this 'dispatch-rider's shoulder'. When he was small his grandfather had told him the story of a samurai dispatch-rider who was on his way to deliver a message when he was suddenly afflicted with this ailment. He jumped off his horse, drew the knife from his saddle sheath, cut into his shoulder, and let the blood run out. In this way, according to the story, he was able to save his life. The details came back clearly to mind. He couldn't let Oyone go on suffering like this, and yet he couldn't make up his mind to take a sharp knife and cut into her shoulder.

Oyone felt dizzy as she had never felt before. Her face was red all over. When Sosuke asked if her head felt hot, she answered in pain, 'Yes, very hot.' In a loud voice he called to Kiyo to put some iced water into an ice-pack and bring it to him. Unfortunately, there was no ice-pack in the house, and so Kiyo brought a basin filled with iced water and a towel, as she had in the morning. While Kiyo cooled Oyone's forehead, Sosuke continued to bear down on her shoulder. Occasionally he would ask if it felt a little better, but she would answer faintly that it still hurt. Sosuke was at his wits' end. He thought of running to fetch a doctor, but fearing what might happen in his absence, he could not summon the courage to move towards the door.

'Kiyo, run quickly to the front street. Buy an ice-pack and then call the doctor. It's early, so he'll still be up.'

Kiyo came immediately. Looking at the clock in the *chanoma*, she said, 'It's 9.15.' She went round to the kitchen door and was looking for her *geta* when by a stroke of good luck Koroku entered the gate. He made straight for his room, without stopping to greet his brother as he usually did, when Sosuke called out loudly to him. Koroku hesitated for a moment at the door of the *chanoma*, but Sosuke called his name twice more in rapid succession, and he had to make a reply. He popped his head through the door. His eyes were bloodshot; it was obvious he had been drinking. As he looked inside, his face registered surprise.

'What's happened?' All trace of intoxication vanished in a second from his face.

Sosuke repeated to Koroku the request he had just made to Kiyo and urged him to hurry. Koroku had not even had time to take off his mantle, but prepared to go out again immediately.

'Sosuke, even if I hurry, it'll take a lot of time to get to the doctor's. How about borrowing Sakai's telephone and asking him to come at once?'

'That's a good idea,' Sosuke answered. As he waited, he had Kiyo change the water in the basin several times, and he continued to apply pressure to Oyone's shoulder and to massage the sensitive area. Since he couldn't bear just to stand by and watch his wife suffer, he found a measure of distraction in occupying himself in this way.

Nothing could have been more painful to Sosuke than this anxious waiting for the doctor to come. As he massaged Oyone's shoulder, he was listening for the sound of footsteps at the front of the house.

When the doctor finally arrived, Sosuke felt for the first time that the dark night would pass. The doctor was businesslike and showed no consternation whatsoever. His small instrument case at his side, he examined Oyone with calm and composure, and as leisurely as if he were examining a long-term patient. The doctor's composure helped to compose Sosuke as well. For temporary relief, the doctor told them to put a mustard plaster on Oyone's shoulder, warm her legs with hot compresses, and cool her head with ice. He himself applied the mustard, from the shoulder to the base of the neck, while Kiyo and Koroku took care of the compresses, and Sosuke took ice from the towel and put it directly on her forehead.

An hour passed. The doctor sat all the while at Oyone's side, watching to see what direction her illness would take. Occasionally he and Sosuke would make small talk, but for most of the time they sat there in silence, just watching for any sign of a change in her condition. The night as always was shrouded in silence.

'It's very cold tonight, isn't it?' said the doctor. Sosuke feeling sorry for him, told him he needn't wait any longer. It would be enough to tell him what to do. Oyone seemed to be much better.

'You'll be all right now. I'll prescribe some medicine. Take it tonight, and I think you'll be able to sleep.' Then he left the house. Koroku went immediately after him to get the prescribed medicine.

After they had gone, Oyone looked up at Sosuke beside her and asked what time it was. The blood had drained from her cheeks, and in the light of the lamp her face looked extremely pale. Sosuke thought it might be because her black hair was now so dishevelled, and he tried to arrange it.

'Do you feel a little better now?' he asked.

'Yes, much better,' and she smiled her usual smile. Oyone seldom forgot to show Sosuke a smiling face, even when she was in pain. Kiyo had stretched herself on the floor of the *chanoma* and was snoring.

'Please send Kiyo to bed,' Oyone requested.

Koroku returned from the druggist's, and Oyone took the medicine as the doctor had prescribed. It was now about midnight. In less than twenty minutes she was sound asleep.

'She's finally fallen asleep,' said Sosuke, bending over her.

Koroku looked for a time at his sister-in-law and answered, 'She should be all right now.' Then they took the ice from her forehead.

Finally Koroku went to his room, and Sosuke spread out his bedding next to Oyone's and went to bed as usual. Five or six hours later the winter night took its departure, leaving behind it spiky frost patterns. An hour afterwards, the sun, giving an orange flush to the earth, rose unhesitatingly into a blue sky that offered it no resistance. Oyone was still sound asleep.

Sosuke had his breakfast, and it was soon time to go to work. Oyone still showed no sign of awakening from her sleep. Sosuke bent over her and, listening to her deep breathing, wondered if he should go to work or take the day off.

XII

At the office that morning Sosuke tried to do his work as usual, but the image of Oyone the night before kept coming to mind, and he started worrying anew about her condition. In this state, the work did not go very smoothly, and he made a number of errors. He persevered till noon, then decided to go home.

On the way back in the streetcar he tried to imagine that everything was well, that Oyone had now awakened from her long sleep and was feeling much better, and that there was no sign of a new attack. At this time of day there were only a few passengers, and he could relax without the nervous strain of the crowded rush-hour. He could leisurely entertain the images that passed through his mind. Before he knew it, the car had reached the last stop.

When he arrived at his front gate, he saw that all was quiet within. It looked as if no one was at home. He entered the house, took off his shoes, and stepped up into the front room. No one came to greet him. Instead of entering

115

the *chanoma* from the veranda, as he usually did, he walked straight through the house and opened the doors to the parlour, where Oyone's bed was laid. He was startled to see that she was still asleep. Beside her pillow on a vermilion tray were a glass of water and the packet of medicine from the night before. The glass was still half-full of water, just as when he had left that morning. Her head was pointed towards the *tokonoma*, her left cheek uppermost and a patch of mustard plaster visible above the collar of her kimono — this too exactly as he remembered seeing it that morning. Just as when he had left for work, she was in so deep a sleep that were it not for her regular breathing she would have seemed to be no longer of this world. Everything, in short, corresponded exactly to the image he had taken with him to the office that morning. Not even allowing time to remove his coat, he bent down and listened for a while to her regular breathing. She showed no sign of waking from her deep sleep. He counted on his fingers the hours that had passed since she had taken the medicine. Then for the first time he began to get alarmed. Before, he had worried about her not getting enough sleep, but when he saw her asleep like this for so many hours, it seemed highly unnatural, more unnatural than her previous sleeplessness.

He shook her lightly two or three times, causing her hair, spread out over her pillow, to undulate gently. But she remained asleep. He left her and went out into the kitchen. Some dirty teacups had been left in the bucket by the sink. He looked into the maid's room. Kiyo was lying stretched out on the floor in front of the little table where she had had lunch. He opened the door to Koroku's room and looked inside. Koroku too was asleep, his head under the blankets.

Sosuke changed, folded his suit neatly, and put it away in the wardrobe. He built up the fire in the brazier and prepared to boil some water. He sat for two or three minutes beside the brazier, lost in thought. When he finally rose, he went first to awaken Koroku, and then Kiyo. Both were startled and jumped up at once. When Sosuke asked Koroku for an account of Oyone's condition in his absence, Koroku confessed that he had been so sleepy that after lunch, which he had taken at half past eleven, he had gone back to bed, but that until then Oyone had remained fast asleep.

'Will you please run to the doctor's and tell him she's been asleep since she took the medicine he prescribed last night, and ask if this is normal?'

'I'll go at once.'

Koroku was back again shortly. He had caught the doctor just as he was about to begin his rounds. The doctor had listened to his explanation and promised to come as soon as he had completed a couple of essential calls. Sosuke asked Koroku if it was all right to let her sleep on until the doctor came. But since the doctor had said nothing more than Koroku had already reported, Sosuke could only wait patiently at her bedside. He felt that both Koroku and the doctor were lacking in consideration. His displeasure with Koroku increased all the more when he recalled the latter's face the previous evening, when he had arrived home and found Sosuke nursing Oyone. Sosuke had first learned of his brother's drinking from Oyone, but observing Koroku more closely afterwards, he saw that there was indeed a certain lack of seriousness in him. He had meant to speak to him, but had so far refrained, out of consideration for Oyone and the pain that such a confrontation of the two brothers would cause her.

If I'm to say anything, thought Sosuke, now is a good time — while Oyone is asleep. Even if the conversation becomes unpleasant, it can't affect her.

He was ready to confront Koroku, when another look at Oyone's face, bereft of all perception, turned his attention towards her. He was unable to think of anything else

117

but his wish to see her open her eyes, and so he let the opportunity pass. Finally the doctor arrived.

His instrument case tucked at his side as on the previous evening, the doctor smoked a cigarette and listened to what Sosuke had to say. Then he went to examine the patient. As always, he first took her pulse, looking at his watch for a long time. Then he placed his stethoscope on her heart, moving it gently over her chest. He brought out a reflector with an opening at the centre, and asked Sosuke to light a candle. Since there were no candles in the house, Sosuke asked Kiyo to light a lamp. The doctor forced open the eyes of the sleeping Oyone and examined them carefully in the light concentrated by the reflector, and with this he completed his examination.

'The medicine was more effective than I'd expected,' he said, as he turned to Sosuke. 'But there's nothing to be alarmed about. If it had had any bad effect, it would have been on the heart, but I find nothing irregular there.'

Hearing these words, Sosuke experienced a flood of relief. The doctor went on to explain that the sleeping drug he had prescribed was a comparatively new medicine, which, unlike other similar medicines, had no harmful effects; also that its effectiveness varied greatly according to physical constitution. Then he prepared to make his departure. As he was leaving, Sosuke asked, 'Then it's all right to let her sleep on until she wakes up naturally?' The doctor answered that unless there were some special reason for waking her, there was no need to do so.

After the doctor's departure Sosuke felt suddenly hungry. He went into the *chanoma* and discovered that the water in the tea-kettle he had set on the brazier had come to the boil. He called Kiyo and told her to set out the evening meal. Kiyo hesitated, then explained that she had not even begun preparations yet. Only then did Sosuke realize that it was still some time before their usual dinner hour. He sat himself comfortably cross-legged beside the brazier. To ease

118

his hunger he chewed on some pickled radish and drank four cups of tea in rapid succession. About half an hour later Oyone opened her eyes.

XIII

Sosuke, deciding to get a haircut to welcome in the New Year, set foot in a barber's for the first time in several weeks. Many others, apparently, had had the same idea, for the shop was crowded with customers. A metallic chorus of scissors echoed through the room with the same restless rhythm he had just encountered on the street, where people were scurrying about here, there, and everywhere in a rush to bid farewell to the cold of the old year and welcome in the warmth of the new.

As he sat beside the stove smoking a cigarette, waiting his turn, he felt as if he too were being drawn, against his will, into the feverish activity of a world to which he did not belong; as if he were being dragged along helplessly over the threshold of the new year. He had closed his eyes to its approach until it was almost upon him, since for people like himself, it could hold out little new hope. All the same, the festive mood of the season was catching, and he could not help feeling some of the excitement himself.

Oyone's condition had finally returned to normal, to the point that he could now be away from home without always worrying about what might happen in his absence. Their preparation for the coming of spring was very modest indeed when compared to that of people around them, but for them too it was the busiest season of the year. This year Sosuke was of a mind to make the preparation even simpler than in past years. When he saw his wife before him as if risen from the dead, he was choked with emotion, just as when a terrible tragedy has been but narrowly averted. At the same time an undefined fear that this tragedy, though

119

once averted, would return in some other form to engulf his family circle remained as a shadow in his mind.

When he saw the restless New Year's rush about him, as people of the world, vibrant with life, sought frantically to thrust aside the few short days of the old year that still remained, his fears increased. It even occurred to him that it might be better to remain alone in the drab gloom of the old year.

His turn for a haircut finally came. He looked intently at his face reflected coldly in the mirror, and wondered who he really was. From the neck down he was draped in the white barber's cloth, with neither the colour nor the pattern of his suit visible. He noticed that the cage of the proprietor's pet bird was also reflected in the mirror, and he began to watch the bird flutter about on its perch.

Sosuke felt refreshed as he left the shop with a nice-smelling pomade on his hair and the proprietor's cheerful 'Thank you' in his ears. As he walked along in the brisk air of the street he was glad that he had acted upon Oyone's suggestion that he get a haircut. His spirits were renewed.

He had to see his landlord to inquire about the water rates, and so he called in on his way home. The maid came to the door. Instead of showing him to the parlour, where he usually waited for Sakai to make his appearance, she led him to the *chanoma*. The door to the room was slightly ajar and he could hear three or four people laughing inside. Sakai's family, he reflected, were in good spirits, as always.

Sakai was seated opposite a glossy brazier. Mrs Sakai was farthest away from the brazier, near the veranda door-panels, facing Sosuke as he entered. Behind Sakai hung a wall clock in a long, narrow, black case. To the right of the clock was the wall and to the left a shelf above which were displayed a couple of scrolls and a decorated fan.

In the room with Mr and Mrs Sakai were two little girls, dressed alike, sitting shoulder to shoulder. One was twelve or thirteen, the other about ten. Wide-eyed, they watched

120

Sosuke enter the room. From their eyes and lips he could tell that they had just been laughing. He took a quick glance around the room and saw that the Sakais had another visitor, a funny little man who sat very stiffly near the entrance.

Sosuke had not been in the room five minutes when he realized that this little man must have been the cause of the laughter he had heard before entering. He had reddish hair, dirty and coarse, and his face was so darkly tanned by the sun that it seemed a lifetime would not be enough to restore it to its natural colour. The white cotton shirt he wore had buttons made of baked clay. From his scarf, made of stiff wadded cotton that had been homespun, hung down two long strings that looked as if they might be the strings of his wallet. His general appearance suggested that he hailed from a far-off mountain region with no easy access to Tokyo. In spite of the cold, the man knelt to pull out a towel tucked into his faded blue sash, and began to wipe his face with it.

'This gentleman has come all the way from Yamanashi prefecture to sell his cloth in Tokyo,' explained Sakai, introducing him to Sosuke.

The pedlar looked at Sosuke and by way of greeting asked, 'How about you, sir? Wouldn't you like to buy some cloth?'

He had all kinds of cloth spread out around him: lengths of ordinary silk, cloth for everyday kimonos, white pongee. Sosuke was surprised that despite his unprepossessing appearance and strange country speech he should have such fine material to sell. Mrs Sakai explained that the soil of the pedlar's native region was of volcanic rock and unsuitable for raising rice, or even millet, so that the natives in desperation had planted mulberry trees and taken to raising silkworms. The town from which he came was very poor. Only one house could boast of having a clock, and only three of the town's children were able to go to school.

'I hear that this gentleman is the only one in the town who can write,' added Mrs Sakai, laughing.

'That's true, lady,' the pedlar affirmed gravely, 'I'm the only one that can read, write, and do sums. It's an awful place, lady.'

He brought out more of his wares, displaying them to the Sakais and urging them to buy this or that. When they objected to the price and tried to get him to lower it, he argued back in his peculiar country idiom and had them all laughing again. The Sakais seemed to have all the time in the world as they continued their cheerful conversation with the pedlar.

'When you're making your rounds like this, what do you do when it's time to eat?' asked Mrs Sakai.

'You don't think I can get along without eating, do you? When I get hungry, I stop to eat.'

'Where do you eat?'

'Usually in a tea-house.'

'What do you call a tea-house?' pursued Mrs Sakai, laughing again.

'A place where you can get something to eat,' replied the pedlar. He had found the food in Tokyo very tasty, he continued, and he ate whenever he felt hungry. For that reason he didn't like to take his meals at an inn, where he could eat only three times a day. At this they all burst out laughing again.

Before he took his leave he was able to sell Mrs Sakai some pongee cloth and material for a summer kimono. How nice it must be, reflected Sosuke, to have the means to be able to buy a summer dress in winter.

Mrs Sakai turned to Sosuke and asked, 'How about you? Wouldn't you like to buy something for your wife?' She pointed out how much cheaper it was to buy from the pedlar. 'You can always pay for it later.' Sosuke decided to buy cloth for a kimono for Oyone. Sakai haggled with the pedlar and got him to sell Sosuke the cloth for three yen.

After he had agreed to Sakai's price, the pedlar lamented, 'This is giving it away. I feel like crying.' And they all laughed again.

The pedlar spoke in his amusing patois wherever he went. As he made the rounds of his customers, the load on his back gradually grew lighter and lighter until finally all that remained was some cloth of dark blue for wrapping parcels and some flat braid. By this time the New Year would be approaching and he would return to his home and spend the early part of spring in the mountains, then would come back to Tokyo again with as much cloth as he could carry. By the end of April or the beginning of May, which was the busiest time of the year for the silk growers, he would have turned all his goods into cash and be back again in his little village of volcanic rock which lay to the north of Mount Fuji.

'It's four or five years since he began stopping here, but he's always the same. He doesn't change a bit,' Mrs Sakai remarked.

'He's really an amazing man,' her husband agreed. In a world in which a person who doesn't leave the house for three days may very well find, when he ventures out on the fourth, that his street has been widened, or who fails to read today's newspaper and discovers next day that the streetcar timetable has been revised, it was all the more remarkable that a man like this, who spent two months of every year in Tokyo, should continue to carry on unchanged the characteristics of his native region. Sosuke, taking in the man's features, attitudes, attire and speech, felt a little sorry for him.

Even after he had taken leave of Sakai and was on his way home, the cloth he had bought for Oyone tucked under his arm, the image of the pedlar, who had sold him the cloth for the very low price of three yen, remained before his eyes. He could still see his plain clothes of a striped material; his shock of reddish hair, stiff and dry, but which,

123

even without a drop of hair-oil, was parted neatly exactly in the centre.

When he got home, Oyone had just completed, at long last, the light spring coat she had been making for him. Instead of pressing the seams in place, she folded the coat carefully, placed a cushion over it, then sat down on the cushion.

'You can stretch it out under your bedding tonight and sleep over it.'

Sosuke told Oyone about the funny little man at Sakai's, and even she laughed heartily. She looked long and lovingly at the cloth he had bought for her, repeating over and over again, 'Very cheap, very cheap.' It was indeed a fine piece of material.

'How can he sell it so cheaply and still make a profit?' she wondered.

'That just shows how much profit the middleman makes,' answered Sosuke, as if he knew all about these things, when in reality he was drawing his conclusions from this one case.

They began to talk about other matters — how well-off the Sakais were; how, because of their fortunate circumstances, they were able to let the local antique dealer make an exorbitant profit off them, and buy at a low price from the mountain pedlar material which they had no present use for; and, finally, what a cheerful and lively family they were.

Sosuke, in a changed tone of voice, suddenly exclaimed, 'But that's not because they have money. It's because they have a house full of children. With children, even a poor home is generally quite cheerful.'

Oyone discerned a note of bitterness in his voice. It was as if he thought that they themselves were to blame for the drab life they lived. Unconsciously she took her hands off the cloth on her lap and looked at her husband. Sosuke did not notice her reaction. He was too pleased at finding her so happy with the material he had brought back from the

Sakais for her. It was the first time in a long while that he had been able to give her a little pleasure. Oyone looked at him for a time, but did not speak. Still, she turned his remark over and over in her mind until it was time for bed.

They retired a little after ten as usual. Looking for her chance before her husband dropped off to sleep, Oyone turned to him and said, 'You mentioned that it's very gloomy without children in the house.'

Sosuke remembered having made some such remark, but he hadn't meant to apply it to their situation, much less to draw Oyone's attention to the fact of their being childless. When his casual remark was picked up by her in this fashion, he didn't know what to reply.

'I wasn't speaking about us.'

Oyone was silent for a moment, then took up the point again.

'But still you must have said that because you think that our house too is always so gloomy.' She said almost the same thing as before.

Something in Sosuke recognized the truth of what she said. But out of consideration for her, he could not freely speak out the blunt truth. His wife had just recovered from a severe illness. To set her mind at ease, he thought it would be better to make a joke of the matter.

'I suppose you might call our home a bit gloomy,' he said, in as cheerful a tone as he could command, but then he was stuck: he could think of nothing amusing to give a jocular turn to his words. All he could say was, 'It's certainly nothing to worry about.'

Oyone made no answer, and Sosuke attempted to change the subject.

'There was a fire again last night, wasn't there?'

Oyone ignored this and in a voice filled with pain cried out, 'I'm sorry that you. . . .' She didn't finish the sentence. The lamp was placed in the *tokonoma* as usual. Oyone had her back to the light so that Sosuke could not make out the

125

expression on her face, but her voice sounded as if she were crying. Until now, Sosuke had been lying on his back, looking up at the ceiling. Now he turned and looked at his wife, peering for a long time into her face, which because of the angle of light, was only a grey shadow. She too stared intently at him.

'I wanted to tell you and apologize. But it was so hard to say and I never got round to it.' Her words came out in short bursts between pauses. Sosuke had no idea what she was trying to tell him. He thought she might be hysterical, but he wasn't sure, and so he waited. Then her words became very distinct: 'There's no chance that I will ever be able to have children,' and she burst into tears.

After this tear-filled confession, Sosuke was at a loss how to console her. Now it was his turn to feel deeply sorry for her.

'We can do without children, can't we? Someone with a lot of children like Sakai — he's a man to be pitied. It's just like a kindergarten over there.'

'But not to be able to have even one child! Isn't that terrible?'

'You aren't really sure that you can't have children. Let's just wait and see.'

Oyone only began to cry all the harder. Sosuke did not know what to do, and so he just waited for her to calm down, then listened quietly to her explanation.

Sosuke and Oyone had succeeded in making their married life together more harmonious than that of the average couple. At the same time, in not having children they were less fortunate than the people about them. If it had been impossible from the first to have a child, they might more easily have resigned themselves to their lot. But to have conceived and then failed to bring the fruit of conception to maturity magnified greatly the grief of their childless state.

The first time Oyone had become pregnant was just after the couple had moved from Kyoto and were living in makeshift quarters in Hiroshima. When she realized that she was with child, Oyone lived through the new experience with mixed feelings of joyful anticipation, and at the same time, dread apprehension, of the future. Sosuke had welcomed the news with great joy, looking upon the child they had created as the realization of the love they bore one another, and he waited eagerly, counting the days until this flesh into which he had poured his life would appear before him. His hopes, however, were not to be fulfilled. In the fifth month Oyone lost her child. The months that followed were very painful for both of them. Sosuke, seeing Oyone's sickly pallor after losing the child, attributed the tragedy to the impoverished circumstances in which they were living. He regretted that their poverty had effectively crushed the fruit of their love before it could see the light of day. Oyone cried her heart out.

Soon after they moved to Fukuoka, Oyone became pregnant again. She had heard that losing one child often meant losing subsequent ones. She was on her guard and was careful in everything she did. The pregnancy, as a result, went very smoothly. Yet for no discernible reason, the baby was born prematurely. The midwife shook her head and urged them to consult a doctor. The doctor who came to look at the child told them that it was underdeveloped. They would have to keep the room at a fixed temperature day and night. Sosuke went to great sacrifice to have a heater installed, and the couple watched incessantly over the child and did all they could to preserve its life. But all in vain: one week later the poor infant to whom they had given of their blood turned cold. Oyone held the lifeless body in her arms and sobbed, 'What shall we do?'

Sosuke bore up manfully under this new blow. The cold flesh of the babe was turned to ashes and the ashes returned to black earth. Still, nothing like a complaint passed his lips. In their mutual grief the dark shadow that had stood between them until this moment gradually receded and finally vanished completely.

Then Oyone became pregnant a third time. It was the first year after they moved to Tokyo. She was still physically exhausted from the strain of moving, and both she and her husband took very great care. They were both determined that everything should go well this time. The tension-filled months of her pregnancy moved along without event until the fifth month. Then Oyone had an accident. At that time they were not getting city water. Every morning and evening the maid had to go to the well to draw water and to do the laundry. One day Oyone had something to say to the maid, who was working at the back of the house. She went out and stood beside her as she did the laundry near the well. In the course of the conversation she went to cross over the wooden drain that carried away the used well-water but slipped and fell on the boards, which were wet and coated with blue moss. 'I've done it again,' thought Oyone. She felt a deep guilt for her carelessness and refrained from saying anything to Sosuke. She waited to see what results this fall might have on the infant she carried. But even after many days, she could still detect no cessation in the baby's growth, and feeling no change in herself either, she was finally able to breathe easily and to tell Sosuke of her accident. He wasn't the least inclined to reprimand her, but merely urged mildly that she take good care of herself.

In this way the nine months drew to a close. As the expected day approached, Sosuke had Oyone on his mind all day at the office. On his way home he would think, 'Today may have been the day. It may have taken place while I was at work.' When he reached his home, he would stand in front of it expecting to hear a baby crying inside. And when he heard nothing, he feared something had gone wrong and rushed into the house. Then he would be embarrassed at his foolishness.

Happily, Oyone finally gave birth in the middle of the night with Sosuke at her side to take care of her. In this they were fortunate. The midwife too arrived early and had the absorbent cotton and everything else ready in plenty of time. The delivery itself was unexpectedly easy. But there it ended. The infant successfully left the confines of Oyone's womb, but it never breathed the air of the outside world. The midwife took out what looked like a slender glass tube and continued for a long time to breathe heavily through it into the baby's little mouth, but to no effect. The body was only flesh. In this flesh they could make out eyes, nose, and mouth. But they were finally unable to hear a single cry issue from its tiny throat.

The midwife had come only the week before and carefully examined the child in Oyone's womb, including testing its heart, and had declared it in the best of condition. Granted that she might have been mistaken, still if the growth of the child had stopped sometime in the course of the pregnancy, the delivery would not have been so easy, and the mother would hardly have gone this long without feeling some effects. Sosuke began to investigate the matter, and he was astonished to discover certain facts that he had previously been unaware of. The child had indeed been in the best of health until the time of delivery. But the umbilical cord was wound around its neck. In such an extraordinary case there is no other way but for the midwife to cut the child free, and a midwife with any experience will skilfully sever the cord in the process of delivery. The midwife Sosuke had called in, if only by reason of her age, should have known this much. But the case was further complicated by the fact that, as occasionally happens, the cord was wound about the child's neck not once but twice. It had not been cut in time to save the baby from dying of suffocation.

The midwife was partly to blame. But more than half the responsibility for the tragedy lay, undoubtedly with

Oyone herself. Sosuke learned that the baby had been in this condition for five months, ever since his wife had slipped and fallen at the side of the well.

Oyone, still weak from childbirth, listened to this explanation and merely shook her head slightly, saying not a word. Her eyes, sunken with fatigue, became misty with tears, and her long eyelashes fluttered up and down in quick succession. As he tried to console her, Sosuke wiped the tears flowing down her cheeks with his handkerchief.

Such was the couple's past history. After so bitter an experience they were reluctant to speak much about children. By reason of these memories, their life together was clouded by a dark melancholy which they could not easily cast off. At times, even in their laughter the dark shadow in their hearts stood revealed to one another. Thus it was that Oyone now had no intention of opening her husband's wounds afresh, and he too saw absolutely no need to go into the matter again.

When Oyone said that she would tell her husband everything, she was not referring to these events of the past which both had shared. When she had lost her third child and had heard from her husband the circumstances of its death, she had felt herself to be the most heartless of mothers. Even though she had no clear consciousness of wrongdoing, still the more she thought about it, the more it seemed to her that she herself had strangled the tiny life, formed of her own, which had lain suspended between darkness and light waiting to be born. Because of this interpretation she could not help seeing herself as a criminal who had committed a terrible sin, and she secretly experienced gnawing self-recriminations that could be shared with no one else in the whole world. She did not reveal these feelings even to her husband.

As after an ordinary childbirth, Oyone remained in bed for three weeks. From the viewpoint of her physical condition, this was a very restful time. But because of her mental state, they were three weeks of tortuous endurance.

Sosuke built a little casket for the dead child and arranged for a quiet funeral. Shortly afterwards he made a small commemorative tablet for it. On a background of black lacquer was written only a Buddhist name, given to the child posthumously. (The parents had never got round to giving it an ordinary name.) At first Sosuke placed the tablet on the top of the chest of drawers in the *chanoma*, and he offered incense before it every evening when he returned home from work. The fragrance of the incense would sometimes reach Oyone lying in the next room, but her sense perceptions at that time were not very keen. After a time Sosuke, without explaining why he did so, put the tablet at the bottom of one of the drawers of the chest. In that same drawer already lay the tablets of the child that had died in Fukuoka and of Sosuke's father, who had died in Tokyo, each carefully wrapped in a cotton cloth. When the family home in Tokyo had been disposed of, it had seemed too much trouble to carry along with him wherever he went the tablets of his ancestors, and so Sosuke had had these placed in a temple and had put into his suitcase only the newly-made tablet of his father.

As she lay in bed, Oyone was able to see and hear everything Sosuke did in the house. Lying there on her back, she felt that an invisible thread of fate bound her to these two tablets, and not only to the tablets, but to the dead infants, who from the beginning had had no more than a shadowy existence for her. Permeating all her memories of life in Hiroshima, Fukuoka, and Tokyo was the feeling that she was at the mercy of a stern, indomitable fate under whose influence she was, for some strange reason, doomed to experience again and again the same sad misfortune with regard to motherhood; and she even seemed to hear a voice at her ear placing a curse on her. All the while she was physically compelled to remain in bed, her ear-drums echoed almost incessantly with the sound of this curse. Those three weeks of 'quiet rest' were in fact three weeks of painful endurance such as she had never before experienced.

She spent a little over half a month in this mental agony, just staring at the ceiling above her. Finally her patience gave out. Lying in bed had become so painful that on the day after the nurse attending her had been dismissed, she got out of bed silently and tried walking about the house. But even then, the anguish that filled her heart was not easily relieved. Though she forced her listless body to move about, what was in her heart remained unmoved. In desperation she crawled once again under the bed covers she had thrown aside and closed her eyes tightly, as if by doing so she could remove herself from the world of men.

Finally the three weeks were at an end, and nature had restored her to physical health. She neatly folded and put away the bedding, and her eyes, reflected in the mirror, stared back at her with a new life. It was just that time of year when the winter clothes are put away and the spring ones brought out. She experienced a fresh, clean feeling in putting away the winter kimonos after months of wear, in exchange for the light kimonos of summer. The succession of pleasant days that mark the boundary between spring and summer in Japan had some effect in picking up her spirits. But this stopped at merely exposing to the brilliant light the darkness that had been festering deep within her. She began to feel a kind of objective curiosity with regard to her dark past.

One especially beautiful morning she saw Sosuke off to work as usual, then immediately left the house herself. It was already the time of year when a woman will not venture out into the sun without a parasol. She walked quickly under the warm sun, and small beads of perspiration gathered on her forehead. As she walked, she recalled that when she had opened the chest of drawers to change the kimonos, her hands had unexpectedly found the new commemorative tablet Sosuke had made for their last baby, which was kept at the bottom of the first drawer. Finally she turned into the gate of a fortune-teller.

Like many educated people, Oyone had a number of superstitions she had carried with her from childhood. But also like many educated people, these superstitions under ordinary conditions were for her no more than a form of amusement. That they should invade her everyday life was quite extraordinary. But there it was. Oyone that day in a very serious frame of mind sat before the fortune-teller and asked him gravely if she was ever destined to give birth to a child in the future, if it was the will of Heaven that she should ever bring up children.

The fortune-teller looked no different from the kind that set up their booths on main streets and tell the fortunes of passers-by for a sen or two. He fingered his divining block, aligning it this way and that. Then with a solemn air he stroked his goatee and sat in reflection for a moment. Finally he looked intently at Oyone and announced calmly, 'You can never have a child.'

Oyone mulled over his words silently for a moment, then raised her head and asked, 'Why is that?'

She expected that he would reflect again before making a reply. But instead, still staring at her, he answered immediately, 'You have done a terrible deed to another. This sin is still working itself out. That is why you can never have a child.'

At these words Oyone felt as if her heart had been pierced. She returned home with bent head, completely dejected. That night she could not even look her husband in the face.

What Oyone had for so long concealed from her husband was the fortune-teller's pronouncement. Even Sosuke, as he lay in bed hearing Oyone's explanation for the first time with the faint light of the lamp in the *tokonoma* threatening to recede into the dark of the quiet night, felt something like a shudder go through him.

'In your nervous condition you shouldn't have done such a foolish thing. Paying out money to hear stupid words! Did you go back to him later?'

'It was too frightening. I'll never go back again.'

'That's good. It's all foolishness.' And he went to sleep.

XIV

Sosuke and Oyone were certainly a most compatible couple. In the six long years they had spent together there had never been even half a day in which their relationship had been strained. They had never quarrelled or become angry with one another. They bought the material for the clothes they wore at the local draper's and the food they ate at the grocer's, but there was little else to bring them into contact with the outside world. They were hardly aware of its existence, except in so far as it provided them with their daily necessities. All that each had absolute need for was the other; the other was all sufficing. Living in the bustling city, they kept the souls of mountain hermits.

It was natural that their lives could not escape monotony. They were not prey to the disasters that fall upon those who live in a complicated society, but by the same token they denied themselves the opportunity to experience directly the variety that life in normal society offers. While living in the city, it was as if they had turned their backs on the privileges accorded to cultured city people. Occasionally they were keenly aware of the lack of variety in their daily lives. They never experienced the slightest feeling of boredom with one another or desire for more than they possessed, and yet each had a clear realization that the rhythm of their lives was too jejune and lacking in stimulation. That they had spent these long years in daily repetition of the same routine, however, was not because they had from the first lost all interest in the outside world, but rather because this world had placed them in isolation, then turned its cold back upon them. They were not left the space to turn outwards and grow, and so they faced inwards and sank their roots ever deeper and deeper. What their life lost in breadth it thereby gained in depth. For these six years they had not sought to establish and maintain a relationship with the world about them, but had explored instead each other's hearts. In the course of time they had succeeded in penetrating deeply into each other's inner being. To outsiders, they were as ever, separate; but to themselves, they had become one, completely indivisible in mind and heart. They were like two drops of oil that have dripped on to the surface of a large basin of water. The drops do not come together to repel the water; it is more accurate to say that the pressure of the water forces them to adhere to each other, making it impossible for either to get away.

Thus locked in each other's embrace they knew a harmony and satiety — accompanied by a kind of lethargy — such as the average couple seldom experiences. Even when they came under the dominion of this languid spirit, they never forgot to call themselves happy. Lethargy sometimes hung a veil as of sleep over their consciousness, wrapping their love in a kind of mist, but they were never in danger of having sensitive nerves touched by an insensitive drill. In short, their compatibility was in direct proporton to their alienation from society.

Though they lived day after day in unchanging intimacy, such as is realized by few married couples, they did not ordinarily refer to the fact. Occasionally, however, they themselves would become aware of how closely their hearts were bound together, and then, inevitably, retrace their steps through the years of intimacy and recall the sacrifice they had made in daring to marry. They bowed down in

135

fear before the terrible revenge that nature had worked upon them, but at the same time they did not forget to burn incense before the god of love for the happiness in each other that that revenge caused them to discover. They had been whipped to the brink of death, but they had found that the whip was tipped with a sweet honey that could heal the wounds it inflicted.

As the son of a man of considerable means, Sosuke had in his student days indulged himself without reserve in the luxurious tastes common to young men of his class. In dress, conduct, and way of thinking, he was the perfect exemplar of the young man of the world of that day. He carried his head high and swaggered when he walked. In keeping with his collars, which were always immaculately white, with his trousers which were carefully pressed, with his stockings which were of a patterned cashmere, his character was worldly and inclined towards all kinds of extravagance.

He was by nature quick witted, but he had little inclination to study. Learning was for him nothing more than a preparation for life in society, and so he had very little interest in the role of the scholar, who in order to accomplish his end must take a step backwards from the world. He merely attended classes and like the other students filled many notebooks with notes. But when he returned home, he seldom bothered to read what he had written or to put his notes in order. Even the lacunae, representing the days he had skipped class, he usually left as they were. He arranged these notebooks neatly on the desk of his room so that they were always in perfect order, and then he left the house. Many of his friends were envious of his easy way of life. He himself was vastly satisfied with it. A future as splendid as a rainbow seemed to lie before him.

The Sosuke of that time, unlike the later one, had many friends. To tell the truth, almost everyone without exception who came within range of his laughing eyes became his friend. He lived his youthful days expansively, an optimist who could ascribe no accurate meaning to the word 'enemy'.

'If you don't wear a sour face, you'll be welcome wherever you go,' he often told his friend Yasui, a fellow student. And, in fact, his face never wore an expression serious enough to give anyone displeasure.

'That's all right for you. You have good health,' rejoined Yasui, who was always suffering from some physical affliction or another. Yasui came originally from the Fukui region, but he had lived in Yokohama so long that his speech and appearance differed no whit from that of a native Tokyoite. He prided himself on his dress, and wore his hair long, parted in the middle. He had attended a different high school, but he often sat next to Sosuke in the lecture hall and occasionally questioned him after class about points of the lecture he had missed. As a result they became friends. This was very opportune for Sosuke, since the school year had just begun and he had been in Kyoto for only a short time. With Yasui as his guide, he soaked up like sake impressions of the new place. Almost every night the two of them strolled about the lively quarters of the town, such as Sanjo and Shijo. Occasionally they would walk through the Kyogoku neighbourhood. They stood in the middle of the bridge and gazed at the water of the Kamo River below. They watched the silent moon rise above Mount Higashi, and Sosuke felt the moon of Kyoto to be rounder and larger than that of Tokyo. When they tired of city streets and people, they took advantage of the Saturday and Sunday to make an excursion to the distant suburbs. Sosuke was delighted to find everywhere about him broad thickets of green bamboo and to discover the elegance of pine-trees lined up in long rows, their trunks red, as if they had been dyed, and reflecting the sun. Once they climbed up to Enkoji Temple and lay at the foot of a painting by Sokui, faces to the sun, and heard a scull working its way down the river in the valley below. To their pleasure, the sound it made was very much like the cry of a wild goose. On one occasion they went to Heihachi tea-house and stayed there overnight. They caught some little fish in the river, which they fixed on a skewer and had the lady of the tea-house fry for them. Even after their meal, they sat on drinking sake.

Under this stimulus of visiting new places, Sosuke for a time felt all his desires satisfied. But once he had made the rounds of the old city and its environs, and had soaked in its atmosphere, everything began to seem quite ordinary. He felt that something was missing. The beautiful mountains and clear streams ceased to make the vivid impression on him they had made at first. He was no longer able to discover a verdant scene with power to cool his hot young blood. And, of course, he was not living at such a pace that the fever could burn itself out. His blood roared through his veins, raising his pulse and making him restless. He sat Japanese-style, arms folded, gazing at the mountains that surrounded the city on all sides, and exclaimed, 'I'm tired of all this. It's all so old!'

Yasui, who had overheard him, laughed and, by way of comparison, told him about a friend's native place, a spot called Tsuchiyama, remembered in the phrase of the *joruri* which goes 'In Tsuchiyama the rain falls'. It was a place where all that met the eye from morning till night were mountains. It was like living at the bottom of a cone-shaped pewter jar. As a result of his childhood experience of the long-continuing early summer rains, Yasui's friend even today was in constant fear that his lodging in Kyoto would be deluged by the water that came flowing down the mountains on all sides. Sosuke thought that no fate could be worse than that of one who had to spend his life in the eye of a cone.

'I wonder that people are able to live in such a place,' he observed to Yasui.

Yasui laughed and repeated something else he had heard

138

from his friend. Of all the villagers who had left Tsuchiyama, the most famous was a man who had stolen a large amount of money and had been hung on a cross for it. Sosuke, chafing as he was in the narrow confines of Kyoto, reflected that such an escapade would seem to be a necessity, at least once in a hundred years, if only to break through the pattern of boredom in a place like Tsuchiyama.

Sosuke's eyes in those days were always in search of something new. Once nature had displayed to him the colour of her four seasons, he felt no need to revive the images of the past year by going to view once again the flowers of spring or the maple leaves of autumn. Wishing, above all, to live life to the full, he found only the living present or the future, which was coming to birth, of any consequence. The fading past was a phantom of such little value that it might as well have been a dream. He had already seen all the shrines with paint scaling off their walls and the temples where mildew had long set in; and he had no longer strength to revisit a history whose colours had already faded. He was still too alive to be able to spend much time on the half-slumbering past.

At the end of the university year Sosuke and Yasui had parted with a promise to meet again later. Yasui planned to go first to his native place, Fukui, and then to Yokohama. He proposed getting in touch with Sosuke so that, if possible, the two could take the same train back to Kyoto. If time allowed, they would stop off at Okitsu and leisurely look round the temple, Seikenji, go out to see the pines of Miho, and even climb Mount Kuno. Sosuke readily consented to this plan and anticipated with pleasure receiving Yasui's postcard.

When Sosuke returned to Tokyo, he found his father in as good health as he had ever been. Koroku was still a child. Revisiting Tokyo after an interval of a year, he was happy to breathe the sultry air and smoke of the bustling city. He even stood on a high place and looked down over

139

the miles of roof tiles that stretched before him. Under the burning sun they seemed about to go mad and create a maelstrom. He reflected that this was indeed Tokyo. All the objects to which the later Sosuke would never turn his eyes, the student Sosuke found inexpressibly exciting.

His future was still a closed bud, unknown not only to others but even to himself. Still, he felt that it would be characterized best by the one word 'boundless'. Even during the hot summer vacation he did not neglect to lay plans for after his graduation. Although he had not yet decided whether he would try for a government position or go into business, he thought it was to his advantage to advance as far as he could even now. He received introductions directly from his father, and indirectly from his father's acquaintances. He got to know men who could influence his future, and he made a number of visits to them. Several of the people he tried to see were out of Tokyo, on the pretext of escaping from the summer heat. Others were not in when he called. Still others, who were extremely busy, gave him an appointment to meet them at their place of business. It even happened that after taking an elevator to the third floor of a red-brick office building and being shown to a waiting-room at seven in the morning when the sun was still low in the sky, he was surprised to find seven or eight people already waiting there to see the same man. Going like this to new places and meeting new people, regardless of the success or failure of his errand, gave him the feeling that a fragment of the living world, previously unknown to him, was becoming part of his experience, and he enjoyed the feeling.

Even when at his father's request he helped with the annual summer airing of the house, he was able to count this too an agreeable task. He sat on the damp stone that lay before the entrance to the store-room, through which a cool breeze was blowing, and leafed with great interest through a guidebook to famous places in Edo, long in the family possession, and a book on Edo glass. Again, cross-legged on the living-room floor, which was so hot that even the *tatami* on which he sat seemed to give off heat, he took the bulk camphor the maid had bought, parcelled it out into little bags, and folded the bags to look like medicine prescriptions. From childhood Sosuke had associated the pungent smell of camphor with the hottest part of summer, when one was always perspiring, with burning moxa, and with hawks gliding leisurely in the blue sky.

The wind blew and rain fell in advance of the typhoon season. Clouds that looked as if they had been smudged with charcoal moved restlessly across the sky. In two or three days the temperature dropped abruptly. It was time for Sosuke to repack his trunk and prepare to return to Kyoto.

He did not forget his promise to Yasui. When he had arrived home, their meeting was still two months ahead, so he had thought no further of it then. But as the day of departure drew nearer and he still hadn't received so much as a postcard from his friend, he began to be concerned. He sent a letter to him in Fukui, but he received no answer. He couldn't reach him in Yokohama since he had not thought of taking down his address.

The night before leaving for Kyoto his father called him into the study and handed him the money he had asked for, train fare plus enough extra to take care of a two- or three-day stopover and his immediate expenses in Kyoto.

'Economize as much as you can,' his father had counselled.

Sosuke listened to his father's words with about as much attention as the average son listens to his father's advice.

'I won't see you until you come back at New Year,' his father continued. 'So take care of yourself.' But by the time Sosuke's next visit was due, he could no longer return home. And when he did eventually get back to his family, his father was already cold in death. Even now, he could not recall his father's face and kind words at this, their last meeting, without being flooded with sorrow at the grief he had caused him.

Just as he was about to leave the house, Yasui's letter arrived. Yasui had fully intended to go back to Kyoto with Sosuke as he had promised, but something had come up and he had to return earlier. In any case, they would meet in Kyoto. Sosuke thrust the letter into his pocket and went to catch his train.

When he reached Okitsu, where he and Yasui had planned to stop, Sosuke got off the train, left the station, and walked down the long narrow main street of the little town, in the direction of the temple, Seikenji. Since it was the beginning of September and summer had already taken its leave, most of the summer visitors had left the town, and the inn where he decided to stay was comparatively quiet. In the middle of a room which commanded a view of the sea, Sosuke got down on his knees and wrote several lines on a picture postcard to Yasui. Among other things, he wrote, 'Since you wouldn't join me, I came here by myself.'

The next day he followed the plan the two of them had made and went by himself to look at the pines of Miho and the temple, Ryugeji. He wanted to have as much material as possible for conversation with Yasui when they should meet again in Kyoto. But climbing the mountain and looking out over the sea did not give him the pleasure he had anticipated. This may have been because of the weather, but more likely it was because the companion he had counted on being with him was not at his side. He was still more bored when he returned to his inn and sat around with nothing to do. He made a quick decision. He took off the house *yukata* he was wearing, threw it over a banister together with his towels, and hurried back to the station.

The first day after his return to Kyoto he was tired out from his journey on the night train and from carrying his heavy luggage, and so he did not leave the house at all. On the second day he finally made his way to the university, only to find that many of the teachers were not back yet, and that the students too were far fewer than usual. He was puzzled at not running into Yasui, who should have returned three or four days before him. He couldn't get Yasui off his mind, and so he called in at his lodging before returning to his own. Yasui lived in a house near Kamo Shrine, in a beautiful setting of trees and water. Just shortly before the summer holidays had begun, his friend had declared his intention to find a room in the quiet outskirts of Kyoto, where he could study better. Soon afterwards he had moved out to this place, which was about as inconvenient as a country village. The house he had decided upon had a weather-beaten mud wall enclosing it on two sides, and it already looked as if it had existed for centuries. Sosuke had heard from Yasui that its owner had been a Shinto priest at Kamo Shrine. Yasui was taken care of by the owner's wife, a woman of about forty who spoke the Kyoto dialect with a mellifluous fluency.

'Take care of me? All she does is prepare tasteless dishes and bring them to my room three times a day,' Yasui had complained. From the day he moved in, Yasui had had nothing good to say about her. Having been to see Yasui on several occasions, Sosuke was acquainted with the landlady who fixed up the 'tasteless dishes'. And she too remembered his face. As soon as she caught sight of him, she greeted him in her usual soft-spoken Kyoto dialect, then immediately put to him the very question he had come to ask her: Where is Yasui? She had received no word from him since he had left for Fukui. Sosuke returned home puzzled.

For the next week, every day he went to school he anticipated seeing Yasui's face or hearing his voice whenever he opened the door to a classroom. And every day he returned home disappointed. The last three or four days his feeling changed from that of impatient desire to meet his friend, to anxious concern for his well-being. Yasui had gone to the trouble of writing to inform him that due to unexpected circumstances he had to return to Kyoto early, and yet after waiting for this length of time Sosuke still hadn't seen him. He questioned all their mutual friends at university, but no one could tell him anything. Finally one declared that the night before he had seen in a crowd of people in Shijo a man dressed in a *yukata* who looked just like Yasui. Sosuke considered it unlikely that this man could have been his friend. But the very day after hearing this — that is, about a week after he had returned to Kyoto — Yasui himself, clad in a *yukata*, suddenly appeared at his door.

Sosuke stared at his friend, whom he had not seen for so long, standing there in this informal dress with straw hat in hand. He thought he detected something in his face that had not been there when he had last seen him before the summer holidays. Yasui's black hair was slicked down with pomade and parted exactly — very exactly — in the middle. He had just been to the barber's, he told Sosuke.

Yasui stayed and chatted with Sosuke for over an hour that evening. In his laboured manner of speaking, in his diffidence, in the indecisive tone of his speech, in his frequent repetition of certain words in conversation, in all this he was changed not at all from his usual self. But he gave no explanation for leaving Yokoyama ahead of Sosuke, nor did he speak of being delayed *en route* as a reason for arriving late in Kyoto. He said only that he had finally reached Kyoto three or four days before and had not yet been out to his former lodging. When Sosuke asked where he was staying, he gave his address. It was a third-class lodging house in the Sanjo district. Sosuke knew the place.

'Why are you staying there? Will you be there for some time?' Sosuke asked.

'I'm thinking of renting a little house somewhere.' Sosuke was surprised at this unexpected announcement.

144

One week after this conversation, Yasui actually did move into a house in a quiet neighbourhood near the university. It was a small house with the dark atmosphere common to most Kyoto houses. The pillars and lattices had been painted red and black, with the purpose of giving them an antique look. Near the gate, Sosuke noticed, was a willow tree, which may or may not have been part of the property, and its long branches, swaying in the breeze, seemed almost to touch the eaves of the house. The garden was somewhat more carefully laid out than Tokyo gardens. Although the stones seemed to be set according to a free arrangement, there was one very large one placed directly in front of the living-room veranda. Before it was spread a sizable patch of moss, giving the impression of coolness. At the back of the house was a huge empty store-house with a rotted threshold, and behind this a bamboo thicket concealed the entrance to the outdoor toilet.

Sosuke visited Yasui at his new house shortly after the beginning of the second term in October. The day was hot with the lingering heat of summer, and Sosuke still carried an umbrella with him to university. Placing the umbrella against the front lattice, he peered inside the house and caught a fleeting glimpse of a woman dressed in a large-patterned *yukata*. From the lattice it was possible to see, though but dimly, quite far into the house. Sosuke stood and watched until the *yukata*-clad figure vanished at the back. Then he opened the lattice. At that moment Yasui himself made his appearance at the door.

Sosuke was led into the parlour, where he and Yasui talked for some time, but the woman he had seen did not enter to greet him. Nor could he hear the sound of her voice, or any other sound. Since it was a very small house, she must have been in the adjoining room, but she did not reveal her presence in any way. This silent, shadowy figure was Oyone.

Yasui spoke about Fukui, about Tokyo, about university

145

lectures, but not a word did he let drop in explanation of Oyone; and Sosuke had not the courage to question him about her. That was the extent of their conversation that day. Sosuke took his leave.

The following day when they met, Sosuke was still wondering about the woman, but this time also he said nothing. Yasui on his part pretended that everything was as usual. Although the two friends had hitherto exchanged views on a wide variety of subjects in a free and easy manner without reserve, Yasui, since moving into the new house, seemed ill at ease with Sosuke, and Sosuke had not sufficient curiosity to try to pry loose his friend's secret. The woman stood in the consciousness of each as a barrier separating them. Another week went by without their being able to return to their former conversational ease.

The following Sunday Sosuke again visited Yasui. He came on business concerning a club of which they were both members, and so it was an ordinary visit from a motive that had nothing at all to do with the woman. Still, when he was shown into the parlour, sat down in the same place as before, and looked out at the tiny plum trees that lined the hedge of the garden, Sosuke recalled with great clarity the details of his previous visit. This day too the house, apart from the room in which they sat, was shrouded in silence. Sosuke couldn't help trying to imagine the young woman who must be hidden somewhere in that silence. He was certain that this time too she would not come out to meet him.

But he was wrong! Yasui suddenly called Oyone and introduced her to Sosuke. She was not wearing a *yukata* this time, as previously. She came out of the next room, dressed as if she were about to go out or had just returned home. Sosuke was not expecting this. Her dress, however, was very plain. Neither the colour of her kimono nor the sheen of her *obi* was in any way startling. Moreover, Oyone, meeting Sosuke for the first time, showed little of the ex-

146

cessive shyness that so often characterizes young women. She seemed to be just an ordinary person, but more than ordinarily silent and circumspect in her speech. Sosuke, finding her as relaxed before a stranger as if she were still concealed in the next room, deduced that the reason she kept in the shadows of the house was not simply that she was shy and tried to avoid meeting people.

'This is my sister,' Yasui had said when he introduced Oyone to him. But a few minutes of conversation were enough for him to realize that Oyone had not a touch of the dialect of Yasui's native region.

'You've been in Fukui until now?' asked Sosuke. Before Oyone could answer, Yasui intervened.

'No, she's been in Yokohama for a long time.'

That day she and Yasui were to go shopping, which explained Oyone's dress and why despite the heat, she was wearing a pair of fresh white *tabi*. Sosuke was sorry that his visit had interfered with their plans.

'Not at all,' Yasui reassured him, laughing. 'We've only been in the house a short time and every day we discover something else we need. We have to go shopping several times a week.'

'Then we can walk together as far as the town,' said Sosuke, rising to leave. On the way out, Yasui showed his guest the other room. Sosuke's eye was caught by a square charcoal brazier with a zinc ashpan, a tea-kettle made of cheap yellow brass, and a brand new wooden bucket standing beside an old-fashioned sink. Yasui locked the door and ran to deposit the key at the house at the back. As Sosuke and Oyone waited for him to return, they exchanged a few words, but of a very formal nature.

Sosuke was never to forget what each had said during those brief three or four minutes. His words had been but the simple pleasantries a man will address to a woman in the attempt to be sociable, as shallow and fleeting as water.

147

How often before this he had found himself in a similar situation and had expressed himself in the same way!

Whenever this extremely short conversation came to mind, word for word, Sosuke realized again how ordinary, even insipid, it had been; and he marvelled that words of so little colour could have dyed both of their futures a deep red. The red, with the passing of the days, had lost its brilliance. The flame which had scorched them had, through a natural process, changed colour and turned black, and their life together had become submerged in darkness. When Sosuke looked back over the past and retraced the course that their relationship had taken, he realized deep within him how this first simple exchange of words had cast a shadow over their lives; and he shuddered to think of the awesome power of destiny that could transform such an innocent beginning into so significant an event.

Sosuke remembered in great detail those few minutes when he and Oyone were left standing together at the gate. He remembered that their shadows were bent so that the upper halves fell upon the mud wall. He remembered that since Oyone held a parasol in her hand, it was the formless shadow of the parasol — and not the shadow of her head — that was cast upon the wall. He remembered that the early autumn sun, already beginning the decline, was beating down on them. He remembered that Oyone, parasol still raised, had gone to stand in the shade of the willow tree, though there was not much coolness to be found there either. He remembered taking a step backwards and noting the contrast between the purple parasol with a white stripe at the fringe and the willow leaves, which still retained much of their colour.

Every detail was still engraved upon his memeory, although there had been nothing remarkable in the encounter. They waited until Yasui joined them from behind the mud wall, and then they walked off in the direction of town. The men walked together, Oyone a little behind, dragging her *zori* slightly as she walked. The men did most of the talking, and even this was only a short conversation since Sosuke excused himself along the way and returned to his lodging.

The impressions of that day remained long afterwards in his mind. Even when he had returned home, taken a bath, and sat down before his lamp, the sight of Yasui and Oyone was impressed upon his eyes, as if it were a painting hanging there before him. After he had gone to bed, he began to speculate upon the exact relationship between Yasui and Oyone, whether she were in fact his sister as he had said. This doubt, of course, could be resolved only by Yasui himself, but Sosuke jumped to the conclusion that she was very likely not his sister. He thought that she and Yasui had given him sufficient grounds for such a conjecture. It was all very strange, he thought, as he got into bed. Then it struck him how ridiculous it was for him to speculate on the matter. Finally he got up and blew out the lamp, which he had forgotten to extinguish before.

Sosuke and Yasui were too good friends to go for long without seeing each other, which alone would have made it possible for the vivid impressions of that day to disappear gradually from Sosuke's mind, without leaving any traces. Not only did they meet every day at university but they continued to visit each other as they had before the summer vacation. Oyone did not always come in to greet Sosuke when he called. About once in every three visits she would not show her face, but remain quiet in the next room as at his first visit. Sosuke paid no particular attention to this. Still, he and Oyone gradually began to draw close to one another. Soon they were intimate enough to joke together.

Now it was full autumn. Although Sosuke had little interest in sightseeing in Kyoto, as he had done the previous autumn, he accepted an invitation from Yasui and Oyone to go mushroom picking, and in the clear autumn air he dis-

149

covered a new fragrance. The three together also went to look at the colourful maple trees. As they walked from Saga across the mountains to Takao, Oyone tucked up the skirts of her kimono, pulled up her underskirt so that it rose well above her *tabi,* and used her parasol as a walking stick. The sun shone down from the top of the mountain on to the water far below, so that even from a distance they could see to the bottom of the transparent stream.

'Kyoto's a wonderful place, isn't it?' exclaimed Oyone, looking back at the two men. Sosuke, too, at this moment thought Kyoto a 'wonderful place'.

It was not unusual for the three of them to go out together like this, and still more frequently did they meet at Yasui's home. Once when Sosuke had come on a visit, Yasui was away, and Oyone sat alone as if she had been abandoned there in the autumn solitude. Sosuke remarked that she must be feeling lonely and stepped into the parlour. Sitting there with just the charcoal brazier between them, they talked far longer than they realized, before Sosuke finally took his leave. Another time, Sosuke was sitting vacantly before the desk in his lodging room, not knowing how to spend the time — something quite rare for him — when Oyone suddenly called, saying that since she was in the neighbourhood shopping, she had decided to drop in. She accepted the tea and cakes he offered her and they had a long, relaxed conversation.

As the occasions of their meeting multiplied, the trees were suddenly bare of all their leaves, and one morning the tips of the high mountains were found to be covered with snow. The shadows of people crossing the bridge were long and narrow as they walked. Kyoto's winter that year was the kind that launches a biting attack with silent obstinacy. In the especially bitter cold, Yasui caught a bad case of influenza. Since his temperature was somewhat higher than usual for influenza, Oyone was worried. But the high fever lasted only a short time, then receded sharply. He seemed

150

to be on his way to full recovery, and yet he was never quite able to make it. A slight fever remained to plague him each day.

The doctor thought his respiratory system might be impaired and urged him to move for a time to better air. Reluctantly Yasui pulled his trunk out of the store-room, packed it, and prepared it for sending. Oyone snapped the lock on the bag she was to take with her. Then Sosuke saw them off as far as Shichijo, and waited with them in their compartment until the train was ready to leave, trying to make cheerful conversation. Just as the train was moving away from the platform, Yasui called out from his window, 'Come and see us.'

'Yes, please do,' urged Oyone, adding her invitation to Yasui's.

The train slowly left a healthy-looking Sosuke standing on the platform, and headed in the direction of Kobe, belching smoke as it chugged along.

The invalid welcomed in the new year in his place of convalescence. He sent a picture postcard to Sosuke after he had arrived and frequently afterwards, and each card repeated the invitation to come and see them. Oyone always added a line or two to Yasui's greeting. Sosuke kept the cards he had received from them in a special pile on his desk. When he returned to his room, this was the first thing to catch his eye. From time to time he re-read them one by one in the order in which they had come, or else he looked over them cursorily. Finally he received a card from Yasui announcing that he was now fully recovered and ready to go home. But it seemed a shame not to see Sosuke's face there before he left. He invited his friend to come out as soon as he received the card, if only for a short visit. Those few words were enough to persuade Sosuke, who was dying of boredom with his uneventful life in Kyoto. He took the next train and arrived at Yasui's that very night.

When the three friends finally met and looked at each

151

other for the first time under a bright light, Sosuke noticed first that the sick man had regained his colour. He looked much better than when he had left. Yasui affirmed that he was completely recovered, and he rolled up his sleeves and began to stroke his arms, in which blue veins were showing. Oyone's eyes were sparkling with joy. Sosuke was very surprised at the lively way in which she moved them. Until now Oyone had always seemed singularly poised and self-controlled, even under the stimulus of colour and sound, and he had attributed this impression to the fact that her eye movements were so restrained.

The next day the three went out and looked at the sea, a vast expanse, flowing out darkly from where they stood. They breathed deeply of the pine-scented air. The winter sun cut nakedly across a corner of sky and began to sink quietly into the west. As it fell, it tinged the low clouds yellow and red, the colour of a cooking-stove flame. Even then, as night fell, there was no wind, only an occasional breeze that set the pines murmuring. A nice warm sun continued to shine for all three days of Sosuke's visit.

Sosuke said he would like to stay longer. Oyone proposed that they do so. Yasui attributed the fine weather to Sosuke's visit. But finally the three packed their bags and returned to Kyoto.

Soon winter and its north wind were moving away to the cold country, and the patches of snow that lent distinction to the mountain tops disappeared and were replaced by a cloak of green that seemed to spring up everywhere.

Thinking back to that time, Sosuke reflected that if the progress of the seasons had only stopped there, if he and Oyone had at that moment been turned to stone, how much pain would have been spared! It began when spring was just beginning to lift its head from under the foot of winter, and it was all over by the time the cherry blossoms had fallen and given way to fresh green leaves. It had been a battle with life and death at stake. It had been like roasting green bamboo shoots, then pressing out the sap. A furious wind had blown up from nowhere and struck down the unwary couple. When they finally picked themselves up off the ground, they saw that they were covered with dirt from head to foot. This they recognized. But when and how they had fallen, neither could say.

The world was without mercy in holding them to account for their sin. But they themselves, before any recognition of moral guilt, wondered instead if they had been in their right minds at the time. Prior to looking at themselves in shame as immoral, they looked at themselves in wonder as stupid. They could find no reason whatsoever for what they had done. It was this particularly that caused them pain. They resented bitterly the cruel fate whose whim had so suddenly struck them down, though guiltless, and had hurled them for amusement into a pit it had prepared to receive them.

By the time the day of exposure arrived to overwhelm them, they had already recovered from their doubts. They came forward of their own accord to have their pale foreheads stamped with a fiery brand and to be bound together by an invisible chain. They clasped hands and realized that wherever they walked they would henceforth have to walk together. They parted from their parents, their relatives, their friends. More terrible still, they parted from society. Or rather, they were abandoned by all of these. Sosuke was also abandoned by the university. He was allowed to resign from college, thereby at least saving face.

Such was the past of Sosuke and Oyone.

XV

With such a past weighing down upon them, Sosuke and Oyone suffered even after they had moved to Hiroshima. They suffered also in Fukuoka, nor was their burden made lighter by moving to Tokyo. They had been unable to enter into intimate relations with the Saekis. And then Mr Saeki had died. Their aunt and her son, Yasunosuke, were still alive, but were so cool towards them that familiar intercourse was impossible. This year Sosuke had not even made his annual year-end visit to their home, and they had not come to see him, either. Even Koroku, whom Sosuke had taken to live with them, had deep in his heart no respect for his brother. From the moment they had moved to Tokyo, Koroku, with the simplicity of a child, had not disguised the hatred he bore Oyone. Both Sosuke and Oyone were well aware of this. During the day the couple kept a smile on their faces, but at night they pondered deeply over their fate. In this way the quiet years moved ahead one by one. This year too was almost at an end.

Already now, before the year was over, the shopping streets were hung with the sacred straw festoons and were lined on both sides with large numbers of bamboo trees that rose above the eaves of the shops and rustled in the cold wind that blew through them. Like everybody else, Sosuke bought a slender pine-tree and nailed it to his gatepost. Then he prepared the usual New Year's rice-cake offering, topped it with a huge orange, and placed it in the *tokonoma* before a rather odd *sumi-e* scroll painting of a plum tree and a moon the shape of a clam. Sosuke had not the slightest notion why it was to be done in this way every year.

Looking over his arrangement, he asked Oyone, 'What in the world does it all mean?'

Oyone was also ignorant of the meaning of the *tokonoma* decorations, and answered, 'I don't know. But it's always done like this.' She went out to the kitchen.

'But is anyone supposed to eat it?' Sosuke continued, as he touched up his arrangement here and there.

That night they brought large flattened rice-cakes into the *chanoma* and began to cut them on a chopping board. Since there were only three knives, Sosuke merely watched. Koroku, with the strength of a man, cut faster than either Oyone or Kiyo, but his slices were irregular in size and shape. Whenever he cut a particularly odd one, Kiyo would laugh. But Koroku kept right on cutting away at the hard cakes, a wet cloth held again the back of the knife for greater efficiency.

'The shape doesn't matter . . . as long as they can be eaten,' he said emphatically. He put so much strength into his cuts that his face was red all over.

In addition, they prepared a couple of other New Year's dishes, but nothing fancy. Since it was the evening of the last day of the year, Sosuke went to call on Sakai to pay his rent and to thank him for his help in the past year. Hesitating to enter from the front entrance, he went round to the back. Through the frosted glass of the kitchen door he could see bright lights within and he heard a number of lively voices. When he opened the door and peered in, a young bill collector — or so he seemed, judging from the pad in his hand — who had been sitting near the entrance, rose and greeted him. Sakai and his wife were both in the *chanoma*. In a corner of the room a tradesman, wearing a coat with the mark of his shop on it, was making little paper rings for decoration, his eyes fixed on his work. Strewn on the floor beside him were leaves of the *yuzuri* and *urajiro* trees, together with rice paper and scissors. A young maid sat in front of Mrs Sakai. Money — both paper bills and coins — lay on the floor, change, perhaps for an account that had been settled.

When Sakai saw Sosuke standing at the door of the room, he greeted him warmly, 'Thank you for coming. You must be very busy at this particular time. I'm afraid everything's in a mess here. Please, won't you sit down? You must be as tired of seeing in New Years as I am. It used to be a lot of fun when I was younger, but after the fortieth time it gets boring.'

155

Sakai pretended that welcoming in the New Year was an onerous chore, but his attitude and expression belied his words. His speech was lively and his face bright. The sake which he had had with his evening meal still gave colour to his cheeks. Sosuke accepted the cigarette offered him and stayed and chatted with Sakai for twenty or thirty minutes, then went home.

Back at the house he found Oyone with towel and soap dish in her hands, waiting for his return to watch the house while she went with Kiyo to the bath.

'What kept you so long?' she asked, looking at the clock. It was almost ten. Kiyo wanted to stop at the beauty parlour to have her hair done on her way back from the bath. Thus even Sosuke in his quiet life found himself the centre of a bit of excitement that quite appropriately marked off the last day of the old year.

'Have you paid all the bills?' asked Sosuke. Oyone replied that the only creditor still to be paid was the man who brought them their firewood.

'Please pay him if he comes,' Oyone requested, taking out of her kimono a man's much-used wallet and a purse, and handing them to her husband.

'Where's Koroku?' asked Sosuke, as he took the wallet and purse from her.

'He went out a little while ago to watch people welcome in the New Year. It can't be very pleasant on a cold night like this.'

'But he's still young. . . .' said Kiyo, laughing. Then she went to the kitchen entrance and set out Oyone's *geta*.

'What part of town was he headed for?'

'He said he would walk from the Ginza to Nihonbashi.'

By that time Oyone had already stepped down from the matted floor. Soon Sosuke heard the door open and close. He sat by himself in front of the charcoal brazier, gazing at the red coals as they turned to ash. He thought of the flags that would wave the following day. In imagination he saw the sheen of the silk caps on the people who would take a turn about the streets. He heard the clinking of sabres, the neighing of horses, and the sound of shuttlecocks. In just a few short hours he would be plunged into the atmosphere of that day of all days in the year that was most designed to renew a man's spirits.

He visualized the cheerful, celebrating crowds that would throng the streets, but among all these people there would not be one to take him by the elbow and make him a member of his party. Like an outsider not invited to the banquet, he was not allowed to drink the wine. But he was, by the same token, protected from getting drunk. He and Oyone in the course of a year encountered only the most ordinary of problems. But at the same time they had nothing much to look forward to. It was appropriate to the general tone of his life, then, that he should spend the liveliest hours of the year in silent solitude, watching over a deserted house.

Oyone got back a little after 10.30 p.m. In the light of the brazier coals, her face had more than its usual glow. Still heated from the bath, she loosened her kimono about the neck so that her nape was showing.

'The bath was very crowded. It was almost impossible to find a bucket, or even a place to wash,' she said, beginning at last to breathe more easily.

It was after eleven when Kiyo returned, with her hair nicely arranged. She popped her head through the door and called, 'I'm back. Sorry to be so late.' There had been two or three ladies ahead of her.

Only Koroku was still out. When the clock struck twelve, Sosuke proposed that they go to bed. Today of all days, thought Oyone, it would be strange for them to go to bed before Koroku returned, and she tried to keep the conversation going. Fortunately, Koroku came in shortly afterwards. He explained that he had walked from Nihonbashi to the Ginza, then had wandered round Suitengu. But when

157

he tried to board a streetcar to come home, they were all packed and he had had to let a number go by before he was finally able to get one.

He had gone to Hakubaten, thinking to take a chance on a gold watch, but since he found nothing he wanted to buy, he bought only a small glass trinket with a bell attached. With this purchase he was allowed to pick out one of the hundreds of machine-inflated balloons hanging there. 'But instead of a gold watch, all I got was this!' and he pulled out of his pocket a package of powdered soap and gave it to Oyone. 'This is for you, Oyone,' he said. Then he placed the glass trinket, which had the shape of a plum blossom, in front of Sosuke, saying 'Why don't you give this to Sakai's little daughter?'

And that was all there was to New Year's Eve for this commonplace family so tightly bound up in its own narrow world.

XVI

Snow fell on the second day of the new year, turning the rope festoons that hung in the streets white. Before the rooftops returned to their normal colour, Sosuke and Oyone were startled many times by the thud of snow sliding off their roof. The sound was particularly loud at night. The path to their house, which quickly dried out after rain, remained muddy for several days. Whenever Sosuke left home, he returned with mud-caked shoes. He would look at Oyone and remark, 'This mud is terrible.' It was almost as if he thought her responsible for the mud. And she would answer apologetically, with a laugh, 'I'm sorry. This is no day to be out.'

'Oyone, with all this mud it's impossible to walk around here without high *geta,* but away from this neighbourhood, the streets are perfectly clean. In fact, there's even dust flying. You feel pretty foolish wearing high *geta.* I think we're about a century behind the times here.'

Sosuke was not so much complaining as merely stating a fact. Oyone watched the smoke of her husband's cigarette curling out from his nostrils. 'Why don't you tell that to Mr Sakai?' she suggested.

'Yes, perhaps I could get him to lower the rent.' But Sosuke did not act on Oyone's suggestion.

Early on the morning of New Year's Day Sosuke had left his visiting card at Sakai's, but had purposely not waited to see him. All that day he had made the rounds of the people to whom he was in any way indebted. When, upon his return home in the evening, he found that Sakai had called in his absence, he felt embarrassed. The following day it snowed, and so he remained indoors. On the evening of the third day Sakai's maid dropped in to say that if they were free, the Sakais would very much like to have the two of them and 'the young master' over for the evening.

Sosuke wondered what Sakai had planned.

'I'm sure there'll be singing,' conjectured Oyone. 'After all, with so many children. . . . Why don't you accept the invitation?'

'How about you going for both of us? I haven't played the New Year's card game in years.'

'I haven't either.'

The couple didn't care to go. Finally they decided that 'the young master' could go for all of them.

'Go ahead, "young master",' Sosuke urged Koroku, who smiled thinly and rose to his feet. Sosuke and Oyone found it amusing to call Koroku 'young master', and when they saw his reaction to the epithet they burst out laughing. Koroku walked out of the spring-like atmosphere of his brother's house through several minutes of bitter cold into Sakai's brightly-lit parlour.

He took with him the plum-blossom trinket he had bought on New Year's Eve, and gave it to Sakai's daughter

159

as a present from Sosuke. He received from her in return, when it was time to leave, a small doll, undressed, that she had won in a raffle. In its forehead was a hollow that had been painted black. When Koroku placed it before Sosuke and Oyone, he told them with a serious face that the doll was supposed to be *Sodehagi,* a character in one of Chikamatsu's *joruri.* The couple could not of course guess why the doll should be *Sodehagi.* Koroku himself had not known until Mrs Sakai had carefully explained it to him. At first he still had not understood. Then Mr Sakai brought out a text of the play and wrote the characters of the pun alongside those of the original line, and told him to show the paper to Sosuke and Oyone when he got home. Koroku pulled it out of his pocket and showed it to them. One set of characters read 'This single hedge might as well be made of steel', a well-known line from the play; and the second set, 'This brat has a black hollow in her forehead.' Both sets of characters were pronounced exactly alike except for the very last syllable. When they got the point, Sosuke and Oyone laughed heartily, a spring-like laugh.

'That's quite an elaborate pun. Whose idea was it?' Sosuke asked.

'I don't know,' answered Koroku, who had already lost interest. Without further conversation he went off to his own room, leaving the doll on the floor where he had laid it.

Two or three days later — on the evening of the seventh, to be exact — Sakai's maid called again and with great politeness relayed to Sosuke another invitation from Sakai to visit him that evening, if he could get away. Sosuke and Oyone had just lighted the lamp and sat down to their evening meal. Sosuke, rice bowl in hand, was saying to Oyone that spring finally seemed to be approaching, when Kiyo entered to announce Sakai's maid. Oyone looked at her husband and smiled. Sosuke put down the rice bowl and asked the maid if Sakai had anything special planned. He looked more put out than pleased at the invitation. The maid replied in some detail. There was nothing special, and there would be no other guests. Moreover, Mrs Sakai was away visiting relatives with the children.

'All right, then, I'll go,' decided Sosuke, preparing to leave at once. Ordinarily he disliked visiting people. He was not a man to show his face at a social gathering if he could possibly avoid it. He did not ask to have many friends. For one thing, he had no time for social visits. Sakai was the exception. Occasionally, even when he had no particular business to see him about, he would go to Sakai's and spend some time chatting to him. And yet, Sakai himself was one of the most sociable people he was ever likely to meet. That a hale-fellow-well-met like Sakai and a lone wolf like Sosuke could come together and find anything to talk about seemed remarkable even to Oyone.

'Let's go to another room,' said Sakai, leading Sosuke through the parlour and along the corridor to his tiny study. Hanging in the *tokonoma* of the study was a long scroll with five large, stiff-looking characters that seemed to have been painted with a brush made of hemp-palm. Below it was a beautiful arrangement of white peonies. The desk and the floor cushions were in perfect order. Sakai stood at the dark entrance and motioned Sosuke to enter. Then finding the light switch on the wall, he turned on the light.

'Just a moment. I'll light a fire.' Sakai struck a match and lit the small gas-fire exactly suited to the size of the study. Then he offered Sosuke a cushion to sit on.

'This is the den I escape to when I want to get away from things.'

Even Sosuke felt a kind of quiet peace sitting here. The fire made a soft, purring sound, and soon he felt a pleasant warmth crawling up his spine.

'When I am here, nothing is wrong. I am completely at ease. Please make yourself at home. This season is always unexpectedly busy, isn't it? Yesterday I had almost reached the point of complete physical exhaustion. The New Year's a heavy and painful burden. But since this morning I've been able to get away from the world. I wasn't feeling well and took a long sleep. I awoke just a short time ago, took a bath, had something to eat, and smoked a cigarette. Only then did I learn that my wife had taken the children to visit relatives. No wonder it was so quiet! Suddenly I began to feel bored. Man's a strange animal, isn't he? But more New Year's celebration was certainly not the cure for my boredom. Forgive me for saying this, but that's why I thought of you . . . you seem to have so little to do with the world and all this New Year's commotion. In short — this too may be an awkward way of putting it, but I wanted to talk to someone who was, well, above it all. That's why I sent the maid to invite you over.' Sakai said all this with his usual ease and fluency. Sitting with this confirmed optimist, Sosuke could forget the past. He even wondered if he himself might not have become a man like Sakai had he been allowed to develop normally.

Just then the maid opened the narrow door and entered. She made a deep bow to Sosuke and placed a small wooden cake-dish before him and another before Sakai. Without saying a word, she departed. On the cake-dish was a country *manju* the size of a small rubber ball, and a toothpick over twice the length of the ordinary toothpick.

'Please, eat it while it's still warm.' Sosuke noticed that the *manju* had been steamed. It had an unusual yellow skin.

'It's not fresh from the oven,' Sakai explained. 'We discovered these at the place we went to last night. We praised them, half joking, and the man insisted on making us a present of them. Last night they were just freshly made, but now they're only warmed through.'

Not bothering about etiquette, Sakai tore the cake apart with chopsticks in one hand and toothpick in the other and began to devour it. Sosuke followed suit.

As they ate, Sakai told Sosuke about an unusual *geisha* he had met at a restaurant the night before. She was fond

162

of Confucius' *Analects* and always carried a pocket copy about with her on trains and to parties.

'She said that of all of Confucius' disciples it was Shiro that appealed to her most. She went on to explain that Shiro was a completely honest man. When he learned something new, he found it hard to go on to further knowledge before he had succeeded in putting the first into practice. The fact is that I know almost nothing about Shiro and was at pains to keep up with the conversation. But I asked her if it were not something like this: a man meets a woman ideally suited to him and he is loath to meet a second ideal woman until after he has married the first.'

Sakai told the anecdote in an easy, light-hearted manner. Sosuke judged from his conversation that he often went to such restaurants but had long ceased to find their atmosphere stimulating. Still, it seemed that for the sake of convention he went as a matter of routine several times a month. Close inquiry would undoubtedly reveal that even so easy-going a man as Sakai became at times satiated and exhausted with pleasure and had to find refuge in his private study to refresh his spirit.

Sosuke was totally inexperienced in these matters, but there was no need for him to feign interest in them. In fact, it was the very perfunctoriness of his responses that seemed to please Sakai. At the same time, the latter found in Sosuke's commonplace remarks hints of a past that was not commonplace. But when he saw even a slight indication that Sosuke did not want to talk about the past, he immediately changed the subject. This was not so much a matter of manoeuvre as of courtesy. Accordingly, there was nothing whatsoever in his words to give Sosuke offence.

Koroku's name came up in the conversation. Sakai had noticed several things about this young man that might very well have escaped the eye of a brother. Sosuke listened with interest, but did not say if he thought Sakai's observations just or not. Sakai thought that perhaps Koroku not only had

163

little head for the complications of the practical world, as well might be expected at his age, but also possessed, and did not hesitate to display openly, the natural simplicity characteristic of a child. Sosuke thought that Sakai might be correct in his judgment, but he remarked that anyone with only a school education and no experience of society would have a tendency to act like a child, no matter what his age might be.

'Yes, and the reverse is also true. A man with experience of society and no formal education will display a very complex personality, but will always retain the mind of a child. And this may be the worse condition of the two.'

Sakai laughed and continued, 'How about letting Koroku live here with me and help out around the house? He may be able to get a little of that experience we've been talking about.' The boy who had been helping out before had been called up after passing his medical examination. And so Sakai was in need of a boy to replace him.

Sosuke was delighted that such a fine opportunity of providing for Koroku had, with the first approach of spring, thus presented itself, before he had even had to face the problem. At the same time, Sosuke, who had hitherto lacked the courage to positively demand kindness and good will from the world about him, was completely taken aback by Sakai's sudden proposal. But he saw at once that by sending his younger brother to live with Sakai as soon as possible, his own financial situation would be sufficiently improved that with a little aid from Yasunosuke he could help Koroku realize his cherished hope of receiving a university education. He told Sakai exactly what was in his mind. Sakai heard him out to the end, then declared it a fine idea. The matter was settled then and there.

Sosuke should have taken his leave at that point, and in fact he actually started to do so. But he was detained by Sakai, who begged him to stay a little longer. The night was long and it was still early evening. He brought out his watch to prove his point. He didn't know what to do with himself. If Sosuke left now, there was nothing for him to do but go to bed. Sakai sat down again and began to smoke some strong tobacco. Finally Sosuke too followed his example and settled himself once again on his soft cushion.

Sakai returned to the subject of Koroku. 'A younger brother can be a lot of trouble, can't he? I have a ne'er-do-well brother that I've done a lot for.' He went on to explain that while his brother was at university he had been far more extravagant than he himself had ever been. Sosuke, curious to know what kind of a future had been ordained for this spendthrift brother by wily Fate, asked Sakai what road he had taken, what he had finally become.

'An adventurer,' Sakai answered immediately. He fairly spat out the word.

After graduation he had, with Sakai's recommendation, entered a bank. But he was not satisfied with that. He kept saying that he must, before all else, make more money. Soon after the end of the war with Russia he had — against Sakai's strong opposition — gone over to Manchuria, with the hope of enriching himself as he dreamed. There he started a large-scale transport operation hauling soya beans by ship down the Liao river. The business failed in no time at all. From the beginning he had had very little capital to invest, and one day when he tried to balance the books he found a vast hole that couldn't be filled. He was, of course, unable to continue. The upshot of the matter was that he lost whatever standing he had acquired.

'I don't know what happened to him after that. When I heard from him again much later, he was knocking about in Mongolia. I had some doubts about his ability to make a go of it on his own. But since we were so far distant from each other, I simply presumed that he'd get along somehow and I left it at that. He did write an occasional letter, in which he mentioned such things as the fact that the Mongolians had a water shortage, that in hot weather they wet down the streets with sewer water or, having exhausted that, with horse urine, so that the place always had a foul stench. But that was the extent of his communication, except when he asked me for money. I'd send it, then forget about him. After all, Tokyo and Mongolia are worlds apart. Everything was all right as long as he was there and I was here. But suddenly towards the end of the year he showed up again in Tokyo.'

Sakai rose and took down a beautifully tasselled object that was hanging on the pillar of the *tokonoma* and showed it to Sosuke. It was a small sword, only about a foot in length, enclosed in a brocade bag. The scabbard was of an unusual green colour, made of something resembling mica, with three silver bands encircling it. Although the sword itself was only six inches long and the blade very thin, the scabbard was thick and had something of the shape of an hexagonal oak club. When he looked at it closely, Sosuke saw that just behind the hilt of the sword two long, narrow sticks had been inserted into the scabbard. The silver bands, then, had the function of holding them in.

'He brought this to me as a present. It's supposed to be a Mongolian sword.' Sakai pulled the sword out of its scabbard and showed it to Sosuke. He did the same with the two ivory-like sticks.

'These are chopsticks. The Mongolians wear this scabbard on their belt. If they chance to come upon some wild meat, they can cut it up with the sword and eat it with the chopsticks.' He took the sword and the chopsticks into his hands and went through the motions of cutting and eating meat. Sosuke watched his skilful charade with great absorption.

'I also received some felt such as the Mongolians use to make their tents, but it's no different from the old rugs we used to be able to buy here in Tokyo.' Sakai went on to recount a number of facts about the Mongolians that he had heard from his brother — that they were very good with

166

horses, that their dogs were lean and sleek like the Western greyhounds, that their boundaries were gradually being pressed back by the Chinese. Sosuke listened with great interest, since everything Sakai said was new to him. He grew curious to know what the brother had finally ended up doing, and he asked Sakai.

'Adventurer!' Sakai answered as before, with even greater emphasis. 'I don't know exactly what he's been up to. He tells me he's been stock-farming and making a success of it. But you can't believe what he says. I've been deceived too often by his big talk. Besides, he's come to Tokyo on very strange business. He's trying to borrow some 200,000 yen for a Mongolian king. He's going around saying that unless he can find the money, he'll lose all trust. I was the first one he got hold of. But however much land this Mongolian king may own, Tokyo's a bit too far from Mongolia to press for repayment of a loan. When I refused him, he went to my wife behind my back and complained that it was just because I was this way that I'd never do anything that amounted to much.'

Sakai laughed, and seeing the interest Sosuke was taking in his brother, suggested, 'How about meeting him yourself? You'll find his dress interesting too. He wears a loose-fitting robe made of animal pelts. I'll introduce him to you. He's supposed to come over for dinner the evening after next. But you mustn't be hood-winked by him. You won't be in any danger if you just sit quietly and let him do the talking. You'll find it interesting, I'm sure.' Sakai pressed Sosuke to accept his invitation and Sosuke was on the point of doing so.

'Will there be only your brother?'

'No, a friend of his who came back from Mongolia with him is supposed to come along. I haven't met him yet, but his name is Yasui. My brother was very eager to introduce him to me, and so I invited him too.'

Sosuke's face was pale as he left Sakai's that evening.

167

XVII

The sin of Sosuke and Oyone cast its shadow over their entire lives and engulfed them, so that they felt very much like ghosts adrift in the world of men. They had a vague realization that deep in their hearts, too deep for eye to penetrate, was concealed a dreadful canker. Yet as they faced each other day after day, they pretended to be unaware of this. And the years passed by.

What gave them the greatest concern immediately after the event was the effect that their action might have upon the future of Yasui. When they had recovered from the initial shock, they received word that Yasui had left university in mid-course. They were convinced that because of them Yasui had been deflected from a promising future. The next news they received was that he had returned to his native region, and then later they heard that he had fallen ill and was lying in bed at home. Each new word of him only added to their grief. Finally they were told that he had gone to Manchuria. Sosuke wondered if he had recovered from his illness, or if perhaps the news of his going to Manchuria was erroneous. Yasui was not the kind of man, either physically or temperamentally, to find Manchuria or Taiwan appealing. Sosuke did all he could to learn the truth. Then finally he was able to ascertain through a connection of his that Yasui was indeed in Mukden. He learned at the same time that he was well, active, and busily occupied. Only then did the couple look at each other and breathe a sigh of relief.

'He's doing all right,' said Sosuke.

'At least he's not ill,' answered Oyone.

From that time the two avoided all mention of his name. They did not even dare to think of him. No matter how grievously they suffered from the pangs of remorse for this sin that had caused Yasui to withdraw from the university before graduating, had sent him back to his native region, and had robbed him of his health, perhaps had even driven him to Manchuria, they were in no position even to begin to repair the damage they had done.

'Oyone, have you ever had faith of any kind?' asked Sosuke.

'Yes, I think so,' Oyone replied briefly. 'What about you?'

Sosuke only smiled a thin smile and did not answer. Nor did he press Oyone to tell him about her own realization of faith. She may have been relieved that he did not, since she had no clear, well-defined experience that could be put into words. The couple had come this far without either sitting on the benches of the Christian meeting place or passing through the gate of the Buddhist temple. That they had finally found a measure of peace was due only to the medicinal powers of passing time, which is the blessing of nature. And if occasionally a voice was suddenly heard as from afar accusing them of their sin, it was too faint, too distant, and too unrelated to earthy daily interests to be the cause of anything with so fierce a name as 'suffering' or 'fear'. Finally, because they had no faith with which to recognize a God or to encounter a Buddha, they kept their eyes fixed on each other instead. Locked in each other's embrace, they formed together a protective circle against the world. Their daily life came to find its equilibrium in an atmosphere of melancholy, and in this peaceful melancholy they tasted a kind of sweet sadness. Neither of them knew much of art or philosophy, and so they tasted this bitter-sweet fruit without realizing what they possessed and without exulting in their state. For this very reason, their experience was far more genuine than that of poets and men of letters who have found themselves in the same condition. Such was the tenor of their lives until the evening of the seventh day of the new year when Sosuke was invited to Sakai's and heard mention once again of Yasui.

When he returned home that night, he said to Oyone

almost immediately upon entering the house, 'I'm not feeling very well. Let's go to bed now.'

Oyone had been sitting by the brazier waiting for him to come home. 'What's the matter?' she asked, looking up at him in surprise.

It was so unusual for him to act in this way upon returning home from outside that she could hardly remember its ever having happened before. She was suddenly overwhelmed by some indefinable fear and she rose to her feet. Almost mechanically, she took out the bedding and began to lay it out according to her husband's wishes. He stood beside her all the while, his hands in his pockets. As soon as the bed was laid out, he quickly undressed and crawled in.

'What's the matter?' she asked again. She was unable to leave his side.

'I feel slightly indisposed. I'll be all right. Just let me lie here for a while.' Half these words were spoken from under the bed clothes. She felt sorry for him and remained seated at his side.

'You needn't stay here. I'll call you if I need you.'

Oyone finally returned to the *chanoma*.

Sosuke lay under the covers with eyes closed, rehearsing again and again in the dark the story he had heard from Sakai. He had never expected to get news of Yasui in Manchuria from his own landlord. He had just narrowly escaped being invited to his house together with Yasui and having to sit next to the latter or opposite him. He had never dreamed that such a fate was even possible until this evening after dinner. Lying there, he reviewed the events and words of the past two or three hours and marvelled at the unexpectedness of their climax. At the same time, he was filled with sadness. He did not think himself so strong a man that in order to topple him it would be necessary to make such egregious use of chance and sneak up on him from behind when he wasn't looking. To dispose of one as

170

weak as he there were more normal means ready at hand.

The more he reflected upon the course of their conversation — from Koroku to Sakai's brother, then to Manchuria, Mongolia, the brother's return to Tokyo, and finally, Yasui — the more outrageous appeared the role of chance. To experience a coincidence like this, a coincidence such as the average person rarely if ever encounters — a coincidence that made alive again the sorrow of the past — he had to be one man selected out of thousands. The very thought of it gave him pain and, at the same time, made him angry. In the dark beneath the bed clothes his breath grew hot.

The wound, which in the last two or three years had finally begun to heal, now began to throb afresh, and the throbbing was accompanied by fear. The scar seemed about to break open anew and be exposed to a poison-bearing wind that would blow mercilessly into it. Sosuke thought of revealing the new development to Oyone so that she could share the pain with him.

'Oyone, Oyone,' he called.

She came immediately to his bedside and looked down into his face. He thrust his head out completely from the covers. Her cheeks were half-illumined by the light from the next room.

'May I please have a glass of water?' He finally lacked the courage to tell her, and he put her off with this request.

The next morning he rose as usual and had his breakfast as on any other day. Looking at her face as she waited on him, he saw that she felt somewhat relieved, and this gave him a mixed feeling of pleasure and sadness.

'You really startled me last night. I wondered what had happened to you.'

Sosuke said nothing, but merely sipped his tea, with downcast eyes, since he could not find the right words with which to answer her.

That day a fierce wind blew from early morning. It stirred up clouds of dust, and even took off an occasional hat. Ignoring Oyone's solicitous advice that if he had a fever, he would do well to take the day off, Sosuke caught his usual streetcar and sat there with eyes glued to one spot, hearing neither the wind's howl nor the streetcar's clatter. When he got off at his stop, his attention was called to the song of the wires overhead and he looked up. Even as the fury of nature raged, a brighter sun than usual had emerged to reign over the scene. The wind blew cold on his legs. It seemed to have almost visible shape as it flung the sand before it and moved in the direction of the moat beyond. It looked like the lines of rain which under its force fell at an angle.

At the office he was unable to settle down to his work. He smoked one cigarette after the other. Again and again he looked out of the window. Each time he looked, he saw a world under the domination of the wind. He was eager to get back home as early as possible.

It was finally time to leave. When he reached home, Oyone looked at him uneasily and asked, 'Is anything wrong?'

Sosuke had to say something. 'I'm just a little tired. That's all.' He settled himself in the *kotatsu* and did not move until dinner time. The wind receded with the sun. In contrast to the day, the night suddenly dropped off into silence.

'Fortunately, the wind has died down. If it were blowing now as it did all day, I'd be afraid to sit here like this. The house can be so spooky on windy nights!' Oyone sounded as if she really did fear the wind, as if there really were such things as spooks wandering about.

'It seems to be a little warmer tonight,' said Sosuke calmly. 'This has been a very peaceful New Year.'

After the meal when he was smoking his after-dinner cigarette, Sosuke suddenly suggested to Oyone, 'How about going to a *yose* for some entertainment tonight?' Such an invitation from Sosuke was rare indeed, and Oyone had no

172

reason to decline it. Koroku preferred to stay in and roast New Year's rice-cakes, rather than go to hear *gidayu*. So they asked him to watch the house in their absence and departed.

Since they arrived a little late, the place was full. They were ushered to the back of the theatre where there was not even enough room to spread their cushions. They could just barely find enough space to sit.

'What a lot of people!'

'I suppose that's because it's spring.'

As they spoke together in low voices, they looked about at the crowd packed into the large room. Some of the heads far below them near the stage were so indistinct that they seemed to be wrapped in a fog of cigarette smoke. To Sosuke these clusters upon clusters of dark heads belonged to people who had the leisure to come to a place of entertainment like this and spend half a night enjoying themselves. Looking about at their faces, he was envious of every one of them.

He directed his gaze again to the stage and did his best to concentrate on the *joruri* that was being performed. But however hard he tried, he could not really enjoy it. Occasionally he stole a glance at Oyone. Each time he looked, her eyes were fixed on the stage. She seemed almost to have forgotten her husband's presence beside her and to be listening intently. Sosuke had to count Oyone also among those he envied.

In the interval Sosuke asked Oyone, 'Have you had enough? Shall we go home?'

The proposal took Oyone by surprise. 'So soon? Let's stay to the end.' When he did not answer, she added, 'It doesn't make any difference.' She was half-ready to do as he wished.

But then Sosuke thought better of it. After having invited her like this, it seemed cruel to pull her away now when she was so obviously enjoying herself. So he managed to persevere to the end of the performance.

When they got home, Koroku was sitting cross-legged in front of the brazier, reading a book, which he held at the top with the cover folded back. The tea-kettle was at his side, the water turned lukewarm. On a tray were three or four pieces of left-over rice-cake, and beside it a small dish containing a little soy sauce.

Koroku rose as they entered and asked if they had enjoyed the evening. Sosuke and Oyone huddled around the brazier until they had sufficiently warmed themselves and then went to bed.

The following day Sosuke was as restless as the day before. After work he got on the streetcar as always, but when he recalled that this was the day Yasui was to visit Sakai, it seemed unreasonable to be rushing like this towards home and towards Yasui. Still, he had a desire to catch a glimpse of him and find out how much he had changed.

The word Sakai had used the other night in reference to his brother — 'adventurer' — echoed in his ears. With this one word Sosuke associated all kinds of desperation and despair, dissatisfaction and abhorrence, personal disintegration and corruption. Sakai's brother must certainly have experienced something of all these. Sosuke tried to imagine what kind of men this brother and Yasui, who apparently had common interests and who had come all the way from Manchuria together, had become. The picture he drew in his head had the strongest possible colouring, keeping of course within the limits of the word 'adventurer'.

Sosuke, who thus built up in his head a context for the word 'adventurer' that greatly exaggerated the pejorative side, realized that he alone must bear the responsibility for what had happened to Yasui. He would have liked to have just one look at him to see for himself what he had become. He wished to be reassured that the real Yasui had not degenerated to the extent that he imagined.

174

He wondered if there might not be a convenient spot near Sakai's home from which he could observe without being seen. Unfortunately he could think of no place nearby where he could conceal himself. If Yasui came after nightfall, it would be convenient from the point of view of escaping observation, but at the same time it would be difficult to make out his face in the dark.

As he was thinking these thoughts, the car reached Kanda. He found it agonizing to change cars as he always did and head for home. He was not up to advancing even one step further in the direction towards which Yasui would be coming. The curiosity that moved him to wish to get a casual glimpse of the man was not from the beginning very strong, so that when it was time to change streetcars it was completely suppressed. Instead he started walking along the cold streets filled with people. Unlike these others walking about him, he had no clear destination in mind. As he walked, the shops turned on their lights. The streetcars too were now lighted. Sosuke entered a tea-house and began to drink sake. Absorbed in his thoughts, he drained off one glass. The second he had to force himself to drink. But even after the third the alcohol had still not taken effect. He sat with his back to the wall staring out blankly with the sad eyes of a man who drinks alone.

At that time of evening there was quite a rapid turnover of customers. The greater part of them wasted no time but quickly finished their meal, paid their check, and walked out. Sosuke sat silently in the noisy room, and when it seemed to him that he had been there twice or even three times as long as the other customers, he suddenly couldn't stand it any longer and got up and left.

The street in front was bright with the light of shops on both sides. Sosuke could make out clearly the colour of the clothes of the people who passed by. Still the light was too weak to illumine the cold expanse that lay beyond the shops. The night seemed to scorn the gas and electric light that sought to dissipate it at each door, and remained as ever vast and black. Sosuke walked on, bundled in his overcoat, which was black enough to harmonize with this dark world. It seemed to him that the very air he breathed was ashen-grey as it made its way into his lungs.

This evening it did not even occur to him to board one of the many streetcars that passed by, clanging bells and clattering busily along the tracks. Unlike the other people on the street, each with a set destination in mind, he simply ignored where he was going. He saw that he was a man without roots, with a spirit that was merely drifting along unanchored, and deep within him he worried about what lay ahead if this condition were to continue for a long time. Until now the adage 'Time heals all wounds' had accorded with his own experience and had been deeply taken to heart. But two nights ago this principle had utterly collapsed.

As he walked through the black night, he thought of his desire to escape from his poverty of spirit. He felt himself weak, restless, fearful, uncertain, cowardly and mean. Under the heavy weight that pressed down on him he thought only of what specific means he could take to extricate himself, and he had dissociated entirely the effect from the cause, the weight from the sin that had produced it. Events had brought him to such a pass that he could no longer think of anyone but himself. He had become completely self-centred. Until now he had confronted the world in a spirit of forbearance. Now he would have to take positive steps to find a philosophy of life, not a philosophy of life that commanded only lip service but one that gave direction to his deepest self.

As he walked along, the word 'religion' came again and again to mind, but receded quickly each time. Like the curls of smoke one thinks to capture in one's hand only to find when the hand is opened that they have disappeared, so the word 'religion' had for him but a fleeting reality.

'Religion' brought to mind *zazen*. Long before when he had been in Kyoto, a number of his classmates went to Shokokuji to practise *zazen*. He had laughed at them at the time. 'In this day and age' he had thought. When he saw that for all their *zazen* they bore themselves in no way differently from others, he had thought their efforts all the more ridiculous. Now he reflected that it might have been from a higher motive than he in his scorn had assigned to them that they had not hesitated to take precious time to go and sit at Shokokuji, and he felt deeply ashamed of his scornful attitude. If it were true, as people from olden times had believed, that it was possible to reach the stage of calm resignation through the power of *zazen*, then he thought that he himself would like to try it. He could easily take ten or twenty days off from work. But the way of Zen was completely foreign to him. He had no good idea how to go about entering it.

When he finally reached home, he looked at familiar Oyone and familiar Koroku and at the familiar *chanoma* and parlour and lamp and chest of drawers, and realized that only he had lived the past three or four hours in an unfamiliar state of mind. A small pan was placed on top of the brazier, with steam rising up from under the cover. At the side of the brazier where he always sat the cushion he always used was placed, and before it was set a tray with his evening meal.

Sosuke looked at his rice bowl, which was turned upside down, and the wooden chopsticks which he had used morning and evening for the past two or three years, and he said, 'I won't have anything to eat.'

'Oh, is that so?' Oyone seemed a little put out. 'It was so late that I guessed you'd probably eaten somewhere, but just in case you hadn't, I thought it best to prepare something.' As she spoke, she took the pan by its two handles, using a cloth to protect her hands, and placed it on the pad

177

for the tea-kettle. She called Kiyo and had her take the tray back to the kitchen.

Always before when something had come up that made him late in returning from work, Sosuke had never failed to give his wife a detailed account of where he had been and what he had done, as soon as he reached home. And Oyone for her part had always waited for his explanation. But this evening he did not feel like telling her that he had alighted from the streetcar at Kanda, stopped at a tea-house, and forced himself to drink quite a bit of sake. Oyone, who still did not know what was troubling him, would have liked, in her innocence, to hear every detail.

'No particular reason. . . . It's just that all of a sudden I felt like eating some beef.'

'And you walked all the way home to give it a chance to digest?'

'Well . . . yes.'

Oyone laughed as if this were funny. Sosuke, on the contrary, was pained. After a pause he asked, 'Did anyone from Sakai's come to call for me?'

'No. Why?'

'When I saw him two nights ago, he asked me to dinner.'

'He invited you over again?' She seemed surprised.

Sosuke put an end to the conversation and went immediately to bed. But as he tried to get to sleep, he felt a great commotion in his head. Occasionally he opened his eyes and saw the dimly lit lamp in the *tokonoma*. Oyone seemed to be sleeping peacefully. Until quite recently it had been he that slept soundly and Oyone who was troubled night after night with loss of sleep. He felt sorry for himself as unavoidably he heard the clock in the next room strike the hours. At first there were a number of strokes in rapid succession. Then later there was just one, a muffled sound that seemed to have a tail like a comet's and remained long in Sosuke's ears. Then the clock struck two. It was a very melancholy sound. As he lay there, Sosuke resolved to find a way to exercise a firmer command over his life. When the clock struck three, he was only dimly conscious of it, and even less conscious when it struck four, five, and six. He seemed to be part of a greatly expanded world. The heavens were like waves, expanding and contracting. Like a ball suspended from a string, the earth moved back and forth in space in an arc. It was all a dream controlled by a fearful demon. He awoke abruptly from his dream a little after seven. As on every other morning, Oyone was kneeling at his side with a laughing face. The bright sun had driven off the black world of his dream.

XVIII

Sosuke entered the temple gate with a letter of introduction in his pocket. He had received it from an acquaintance of a fellow clerk at the office. In the streetcar on his way to and from work, this man would pull a copy of the *Saikontan* out of his pocket and begin to read. Sosuke, who up to now had had no interest in Zen, did not know anything about the *Saikontan*. One day when he happened to be sitting next to this colleague on the streetcar, he had inquired about the book and the latter had shown it to him. It was a small book with a yellow cover. Sosuke had asked what it was about. The man seemed to be at a loss to explain it in a few words and had answered only that it was about Zen. Sosuke had not forgotten this incident.

Just four or five days before receiving the letter of introduction, he had gone up to this colleague and asked him if he practised Zen. The man looked startled, especially when he saw the earnestness with which the question was put. He answered that he didn't practise Zen but read books about it out of general interest, and he had pulled himself away as quickly as possible. Sosuke had returned to his desk with disappointment written all over his face.

That very day the two chanced once again to take the same streetcar home from work. Having noted Sosuke's earlier disappointment at his answer the colleague seemed to have realized that there was more in the question than an attempt to make conversation, and he now began to speak to him more affably about Zen. But he confessed that he himself had never been to a Zen temple. If Sosuke wished to learn more, he could introduce him to a friend of his who often went to Kamakura. Right there in the streetcar Sosuke took down the name and address of this friend, and the next day, with a note from his colleague in his pocket, he went out of his way to visit him. The letter of introduction had been written there on the spot.

He decided to take ten days off from work on the pretext of illness. With Oyone, too, he pretended to be ill so that she would not grasp his true motive.

'There's something wrong with my lungs. I'm going to take a week off and go somewhere to rest.' Since Oyone herself had come to the conclusion that something had been wrong with him recently and had him constantly on her mind, she was happy that he had broken through his usual indecisiveness to reach this decision. Still, she was taken aback by the suddenness of his proposal.

'Rest? But where will you go?' She tried, but only half-successfully, to conceal her astonishment.

'I thought of going somewhere around Kamakura,' Sosuke answered calmly. Oyone could not help smiling. Sosuke in his plainness and Kamakura with its life and colour did not seem to go together. It seemed funny to mention the two in the same breath.

'Quite the playboy, aren't you. Won't you take me with you?' But Sosuke was in no mood to appreciate his devoted wife's humour. With a very serious face he explained his plan.

'I'm not going in order to spend money. I only want to stay at a Zen temple for a week or ten days of complete rest. I don't know if it will help me or not, but everyone says that a week in the fresh air of the country can be the best of all cures.'

'Oh, that's a different story. Go, by all means. I was only joking.'

Oyone was sorry for having teased her husband who was so good to her.

The next day Sosuke put the letter of introduction in his pocket and boarded a train for Kamakura at Shimbashi. On the envelope of the letter was written the name Mr Gido.

'Until recently he was only an acolyte, but I heard that just a short time ago he was given his own hermitage at the monastery. Look him up as soon as you arrive. I believe his hermitage is No. 1.' The terms 'acolyte', 'hermitage', and 'monastery' sounded strange to Sosuke's ear, but he had thanked the man, received the letter, and returned home.

The lane beyond the temple gate was lined with towering cryptomeria trees, so tall that they blocked out the sky and enveloped the lane in darkness. As he stepped into their shade, Sosuke perceived at once the difference between the world of the temple and the world outside. Standing near the gate he felt a kind of chill go through him, much like the first warning symptom of an approaching cold.

He began to walk down the lane. There were temple buildings on both sides, and also straight ahead; but there was not a soul in sight. The temple grounds had an air of desolation; the verdigris of ages seemed to lie thick upon them. Wondering to which of the many buildings he should go to ask the whereabouts of the monk to whom his letter of introduction was addressed, he stood in the middle of the lane, which he had all to himself, and looked about in every direction.

The temple compound seemed to cut into the foot of the mountain and then climb some little distance beyond. Tall trees screened off the view. The sides of the lane also seemed to rise up into a mountain or hill. The land had not the look of being level. Sosuke caught sight of two or three hermitages, each with its own gate, built on more elevated ground and reached by a flight of stone steps. On the level ground were a number of areas encircled by tall hedges, and when Sosuke drew near to have a closer look, he found that here too each hedge enclosed a small hermitage with the name and number written on a plaque beneath the gate-tiles.

Sosuke walked up and read the names on two or three of the plaques, which were old and weather-beaten. He looked for No. 1. If, when he found it, it did not carry the name of the monk he wished to meet, he thought it would be quickest to inquire at the main temple. He retraced his steps and proceeded to investigate the name and number of each hermitage, beginning from the temple gate. He found the one he was looking for close to the gate on one of the hills to the right. It was built on the very edge of the hill, so that it got much sun. It seemed to be nestled warmly in a pocket of the mountain that rose above it, and it looked as if it might be a good place to withstand the asault of winter.

Sosuke opened the door and stepped inside. He walked along the dirt floor as far as the monk's living quarters and called out. But no one came out to greet him. He stood and waited for some time, but he could hear no sound within. Thinking this strange, he went out and was walking back towards the hermitage gate when he caught sight of a monk with a freshly-shaven head, blue-tinged in the sun, coming up the stone steps. He looked young, hardly more than twenty-four or twenty-five, and had a pale face. Sosuke stood and waited for him at the door of the gate.

'I wonder if this is where Mr Gido lives,' inquired Sosuke.

'I am Gido,' the young monk replied. Sosuke was surprised, but at the same time pleased. He took out his letter and handed it to the monk, who opened and read it on the spot. Then he refolded it and put it back into the envelope.

'You are most welcome.' He greeted Sosuke with great politeness and led him into the house. They took off their *geta* on the dirt floor and entered a room with a large fireplace in the middle. Gido took off the plain, light upper garment he wore over his grey cotton robe and hung it on a nail.

'You must be cold,' said the monk, and he dug into the fireplace and raked out some hot coals that had been banked in the ashes. The monk had a serene manner of speech that belied his youth. There was something almost feminine about the way he spoke in a low voice and then smiled. Sosuke wondered what had moved this young man to take so decisive a step as to shave his head and adopt this manner of life. Observing his gentle grace, he could not help feeling sorry for him.

'It seems very quiet here today. Is everyone away?'

'Not only today. I'm the only one who lives here. When I have to go out, I simply go and let the place take care of itself. In fact, I came back just now from a short errand. I'm sorry I wasn't here to receive you when you arrived.' Thus did Gido offer his guest formal apology for his absence.

Caring for this large hermitage all by himself must entail a lot of work, reflected Sosuke. It would be quite an imposition for him to add to the monk's burden.

Gido read Sosuke's thoughts. 'Please don't hesitate to make yourself at home. After all, it's all for the sake of the Way,' he said invitingly. Then he told Sosuke that there was with him at present another layman who was under his care. This layman had been on the mountain for two years already. When Sosuke met him for the first time several days later, he seemed to be a very light-hearted man, but with the face of an Arhan, emaciated with bulging eyes. When Sosuke first saw him, he was carrying three or four huge radishes which he said he had bought as a special dinner treat. He had Gido boil them, and invited him and Sosuke to join in the meal. Since the man had the face of a monk, he sometimes mixed in with the monks at the main temple or went with them to the village to beg for food. Gido laughed as he mentioned this to Sosuke.

Sosuke heard that there were a number of other laymen who like himself had come to the mountain to do *zazen*. Among these was a man whose trade was selling Indian ink. With a full load of his wares on his back, he would go about peddling his ink for twenty or thirty days and when he was almost sold out he would return to the mountain and resume his *zazen*. Then afer a time when his food supply had run out, he left the temple once more with his ink on his back. He repeated this cycle time and time again and never wearied of it.

Comparing the lives of these people, which at a glance seemed so uncomplicated, with his own, so full of inner turmoil, Sosuke was amazed at the huge chasm that lay between the two. He wondered if they were able to do *zazen* because they were so light-hearted, or if the light-heartedness were the consequence of doing *zazen*.

'You mustn't go about this half-heartedly. If *satori* could be achieved so easily, you wouldn't find monks wandering about the country for twenty or thirty years in the arduous pursuit of it,' Gido warned him.

Gido gave Sosuke general instructions on how to do *zazen*. The *roshi* would give him a *koan* and he must tackle that *koan* with all his strength. Morning, evening, night, and noon he must fight with this *koan*. Gido's words of advice made Sosuke feel uneasy.

'Now I'll take you to your room,' Gido said finally, rising from his place.

They left the room with the fireplace and walked round the main hall to a room on the other side. Gido stepped on to the veranda, opened the *shoji* leading to a rather small room, and showed Sosuke inside. For the first time, Sosuke had the feeling of one who had come from a distance. But, whether as a reaction to the perfect stillness dominating the room or for some other reason, he was in greater turmoil now than when he had been in the city.

After about an hour had passed, according to his reckoning, he heard Gido's footsteps returning from the direction of the main hall.

'The *roshi* will see you. If you are ready, I'll take you to him,' said Gido, kneeling politely at the entrance to the room.

The hermitage was left once again with no one to watch over it as the two departed together. When they had walked some distance along the lane from the temple gate, Sosuke saw a lotus pond on the left. Since it was winter, there was only stagnant, muddy water in the pond and nothing whatsoever to suggest purity or undefilement. On the opposite side of the pond was a house with a banistered veranda that extended right back to a high rocky cliff. It had the elegance of a *Nanshu* painting.

'That's where the *roshi* lives,' said Gido, pointing to the house, which seemed comparatively new. They passed in front of the pond, stopped briefly to look up at the widely-expanding roof, then climbed the five or six stone steps leading up to the house. At the top they went round to the left side. When they reached the main entrance, Gido excused himself and went on alone to the back. He came out shortly and showed Sosuke to the *roshi*'s room.

The roshi seemed to be a man of about fifty. He had a glowing face, swarthy and tinged with red. There was a firmness about his skin and muscles, as if he had his whole body under strict control. He reminded Sosuke of a bronze statue. Only in his lips, which were a little too thick, was there any sign of slackness. To make up for this, there shone forth from his eyes a fire not to be found in those of the ordinary man. To Sosuke, meeting his gaze for the first

185

time, it was like the sudden flash of a cold sword blade in the dark.

'I suppose it doesn't make much difference what you begin with,' the *roshi* told Sosuke. 'How about trying to work on "What was my Face before my parents were born"?'

Sosuke did not understand what he meant, but he judged that the *roshi* wanted him to find out who he really was, to grasp his essential self. He had too little knowledge of Zen to put any further question, and so he remained silent and returned with Gido to the hermitage.

As they were taking their evening meal, Gido explained to Sosuke that the *roshi* could be seen mornings and evenings and that the sermons were given in the morning.

'You probably won't experience any insights this evening. I'll take you to him tomorrow morning or tomorrow night,' Gido said kindly, and he counselled Sosuke to take it easy at first. Since it was very hard at the beginning to sit for a long stretch, he should light an incense stick and measure his period of sitting by it, relaxing himself between sticks.

Sosuke left the room with incense sticks in his hand, passed the main hall, entered the room that had been assigned him, and casually took up the sitting position for *zazen*. But in his present mood this thing called a *koan* seemed something totally irrelevant. It was as if he had come for relief from a stomach-ache and had been offered a difficult mathematics problem with the advice, 'I suppose you might think about this for a time'. Asked to work out the problem, he could probably succeed in doing so, but only after the stomach-ache had improved a bit.

Still, he had taken leave from work and had gone to the trouble of coming all this distance to the temple. Besides, his colleague had done him the favour of getting him a letter of introduction, and Gido was going out of his way to take care of him. Therefore, he had to give it all he had. He resolved to summon up all the fortitude he still possessed and come to grips with the *koan*. He had no idea where this would take him, what effects the sitting would have on his spirit. Entranced by the magic sound of the word *satori*, he set out upon an adventure that was different from anything he had ever experienced in his ordinary life. If by chance he should succeed he even had the fleeting hope that his present troubled, weak, irresolute self might be rescued.

He lit a slender incense stick and planted it in the ashes of the cold brazier. Then he sat down on his cushion and worked his legs into the half-lotus position, as he had been taught. While it was still day, he had not noticed it so much; but now that the sun had set, his room was suddenly very cold. The cold as he sat was so severe that he felt shivers run up and down his spine.

He meditated. But his meditation consisted of vagrant imaginings that failed to grasp either the proper method of meditation or the real nature of the problem he was to attack. It even occurred to him as he sat there trying to meditate that this was all very silly. It was as if a man on his way to visit a friend whose house had burned down, instead of opening a detailed map and checking the exact location, were to rush off in any direction, not knowing where he was going.

Many things flowed into his mind. Some of these he saw clearly, as if they were there before his eyes. Others moved about confusedly, as in a cloud. He didn't know whence they came or whither they went. He saw only that the first disappeared to be succeeded immediately by others, following on without interruption. The thoughts and images passing through his head were boundless, innumerable, inexhaustible, and beyond his power to control. The more he tried to cut them off, the more energetically they gushed forth.

Sosuke became frightened and, quickly recalling his everyday self, looked about the room, whose features could only just be made out in the dimming light. The incense standing in the ashes was only half burned. Sosuke had never noticed before the frighteningly slow passage of time.

He began to meditate aagin. This time objects of all colours and shapes began to pass through his head. Like an army of ants they crawled by, one after another in an unending line. Only his body was motionless; his mind was painfully active, almost unbearably so.

Then his body, positioned there without movement, began to ache, starting at the kneecaps. Little by little his spine, which he had been holding rigidly straight, began to bend forward. With both hands he took hold of the instep of his left foot and released it from its folded position. With no particular aim in mind, he stood up in the middle of the room. He would have liked to open the *shoji,* go outside, and run round and round in front of the gate. The night was perfectly still. It was as if there were no other human being, asleep or awake, anywhere about. He lost the courage to venture out of his room, but he was still more afraid to remain there and be tortured by his vagrant imagination.

He resolutely lit another stick of incense. He repeated approximately the same sequence as before. Finally he decided that if meditation were the aim, then it was just as easy to meditate lying down as sitting. He stretched out the grubby quilts that were folded in a corner of the room and crawled into them. He had no sooner done so than, fatigued by the events of the day, he fell into a deep sleep, without having had even a moment to meditate.

When he opened his eyes, the *shoji* at his pillow were already light, and he saw the colour of the new day creep on to their white paper. Just as it was not necessary at this mountain temple to have anyone watch over the place in one's absence during the day, so at night Sosuke had heard no sound of *amado* being put in place or of gates being locked. No sooner did he realize that he was not lying in his own dark room at the foot of Sakai's cliff than he

188

jumped up. Going out on to the veranda, he saw a huge cactus beyond the rail. He passed in front of the statue of Buddha in the main hall and entered the *chanoma* of the day before, the room with the fireplace. Gido's cloak was still hanging on the bent nail. Gido himself was squatting in front of the cooking-stove in the kitchen, lighting a fire.

Seeing Sosuke, Gido said 'Good Morning' very courteously. 'I came over earlier to invite you to go to the main temple with me, but you were sleeping so soundly that I went alone.'

In this way Sosuke learned that the young monk had already gone at dawn to do his meditation at the main temple and was now back preparing breakfast.

While energetically putting firewood on the fire with his left hand, Gido held in his right a book with a black cover which he read in the intervals of his work. Sosuke asked the name of the book. It had the difficult title of *Hekigan-shu*. It occurred to Sosuke that rather than immerse himself in aimless thought and tire his brain as he had the night before, it might be quicker and more effective to borrow a book on the Way and read up on it. When he expressed this sentiment to Gido, however, the latter rejected this option in no uncertain terms.

'It's very bad to read books. The plain truth is that there is probably no greater obstacle to enlightenment than reading. Even those of us who have made a little progress read books like the *Hekigan-shu* without understanding much. When we get beyond the level of our experience we are completely at sea. Should one get the habit of putting his own subjective interpretations on the passages he does not understand, he will be handicapped considerably when he sits in *zazen*. He will not be satisfied with the stage he is at but will anticipate the next and wait impatiently for *satori* to come. The result is that for want of proper application at his present level, his way becomes obstructed. Reading can thus be a real poison. So I advise you not to attempt it.

189

If you feel you must read a book on Zen, then I would recommend something like *Zenkan sakushin*, which will inspire you to make your best efforts and give you courage to go ahead. Of course, this work has nothing to say about the Way itself; it is read only for the sake of stimulus.'

Sosuke could understand very little of what Gido was saying. Standing before this youthful monk with the blue shaved head, he felt as if he were nothing more than a backward child. His self-conceit, after the events in Kyoto, had long since evaporated. In his life to the present he had accepted mediocrity as his lot. Nothing was further from his thoughts than hope of worldly fame or success. He stood there before Gido as he actually was, without the protection of a mask. Moreover, he could not fail to recognize that he was at this moment even more of a helpless, incompetent infant than in his ordinary life. This was a new discovery for him. At the same time it was a discovery that killed off at one blow what still remained of self-esteem.

While Gido put out the fire in the stove and steamed the rice, Sosuke went outside through the kitchen door, walked over to the well in the garden, and washed his face. Immediately before him was a mountain covered with trees. On the more level ground at its foot a vegetable garden had been planted. Sosuke walked down to the garden, exposing his hair, which was still wet, to the cold air. There at the foot of the mountain he found a giant cave. He stood before it for a time, peering into its dark opening. When he finally returned to the *chanoma*, he found a warm fire in the fireplace and heard the sound of water boiling in the tea-kettle.

'I'm sorry to be so late with breakfast, but you see I have no one to help me here. I'll have it ready in a moment. I'm afraid that in a place like this there's not much to eat. I'll make it up to you by heating water for a bath tomorrow,' apologized Gido. Sosuke was thankful to sit in front of a cheerful fire and have his breakfast.

At the end of the meal Sosuke returned to his room, sat

down, and fixed his eyes once again on the impossible question of what he had been before his parents were born. But since it was a problem without a thread of logic — that is, a problem that permitted no orderly method of approach, he was unable to find a place to catch hold of it, no matter how hard he meditated. Under these conditions he soon grew tired of meditating. He suddenly remembered that he must write to Oyone and tell her of his arrival here. As if pleased to discover some ordinary task that had to be done, he took out some paper and an envelope from his bag and began at once. He told her first about the tranquillity of the temple, about its being warmer here than in Tokyo, perhaps because of the proximity of the sea, about the freshness of the air, about the kindness of the monk to whom he had brought a letter of introduction, about the bad food, the grubby quilts, and so on, until it became quite a long letter. Then he put aside his pen. He did not tell her — or even give her reason to guess — how he was agonizing over the *koan*, how his joints were hurting him as he did *zazen*, or how because of his meditation his nerves seemed to be getting more on edge than they were before. He stuck a stamp on the envelope and, on the pretext of having to drop it into the post, went down off the mountain at once. He wandered about the village for a while, oppressed by thoughts of his face before the birth of his parents, of Oyone, and of Yasui; and then he returned to the hermitage.

At noon the layman Gido had told Sosuke about earlier appeared. He took out his rice dish and had Gido fill it. He spoke not a word. He merely folded his hands in the conventional position of thanks and expressed everything necessary in gestures. It was a rule here, apparently, to remain as silent as possible. Abstention from speaking, or even from making noise, was in accord, it seemed, with the spirit of not placing any obstacle to meditation. Looking over his actions and attitude since the previous evening in the light of this severe application to the Way, Sosuke could not help being ashamed of himself.

After the meal the three sat around the fireplace and talked for a time. The layman said that he sometimes fell asleep while doing *zazen*, and just before he returned to full consciousness he had the experience on occasion of feeling with joy that he had achieved *satori*. But when his eyes finally opened, he discovered that he was still his usual self and a deep discouragement would come upon him. Sosuke laughed. He felt more relaxed to know that there were people following the Way who were so light-hearted. When the three broke up to go to their own rooms, Gido said to Sosuke, 'I invite you to go to the main temple with me tonight. But please apply yourself earnestly to your sitting until evening.' This firm recommendation, too, caused Sosuke to feel a kind of responsibility. He returned to his room with the uncomfortable feeling one has when undigested dumplings are clogging the stomach. He lit a stick of incense and took up once again his sitting position. For all his good resolutions, however, he was unable to remain sitting until evening. Despite the pressure to find some kind of answer to the *koan*, whatever it might be, his patience finally gave out and all that he had on his mind was the desire for Gido to come quickly from the main hall to tell him that supper was ready.

He was in anguish and fatigue as he watched the sun begin to decline. As the shadows that fell across his *shoji* began to grow dimmer and to disappear, the air of the temple, starting from beneath the floor boards, grew chilly. From morning there had been no wind in the trees. When he stepped out on to the veranda and looked up at the high roof, he saw a long line of black tiles whose edges were exactly aligned, and beyond that a calm sky whose blue light was gradually moving downwards and growing dim.

XIX

'Be careful. It's dangerous,' said Gido, going down the stone steps in the dark with Sosuke immediately behind him. Here, in contrast to the city, the night was pitch black, and Gido lit a lantern to light even the short distance they had to go. Once off the steps, they stood under huge trees whose branches extended widely to right and left, cutting off the sky. Although it was dark, the colour of the green needles made Sosuke feel cold, almost as if they had been able to penetrate through the weave of his kimono. Even in the weak light of the lantern, Sosuke fancied he could make out their colour. The lantern — and the light flowing out from it — seemed very puny, perhaps because he could imagine the huge size of the tree trunks. It illuminated only the small circle about them, an area of grey cut out of the dark that surrounded it, moving along with their shadows.

The place beyond the pond where they had to climb up to the left was slippery and a little hard to manage, especially for Sosuke who was coming here for the first time at night. He had trouble with his *geta* a couple of times. There was a back way which cut directly across before reaching the pond, but Gido, thinking that despite the shorter distance this would be less convenient for Sosuke who did not know the way, took him by the main path.

There were many *geta* lined up at the entrance. Sosuke was careful not to disturb them as he stepped up into a room which was just a little larger than his room at the hermitage. Six or seven men were lined up along the wall on one side. Among them were a couple of priests with black robes and shining shaved heads. Most of the others were dressed in *hakama*. Leaving an opening near the entrance for others to pass, they sat in an orderly line around the room making an L-shape. They spoke not a word. One look at their faces was enough to impress Sosuke, first of all, with their air of austerity. They sat there with lips pursed and eyebrows knit portentously. They did not look about to see who was beside them, nor did they even seem to notice who came through the door. They had the bearing of living statues as they sat with rigid backs in this room that was without heat. The cold of the mountain temple thus acquired for Sosuke a kind of solemn, ceremonial aspect.

After a time the stillness was broken by the sound of footsteps. Far off and faint at first, they began to echo loudly as they approached the place where Sosuke was sitting. A priest suddenly appeared from the corridor. He passed by Sosuke and went out into the dark of the night. Then from somewhere deep in the bowels of the temple came the sound of a gong.

At the sound, one of the men sitting in the solemn line rose, this too without saying a word, and walked to the corner of the room opposite the corridor and sat down again. There, in a frame in the corner a gong was hanging, much heavier and thicker than the average. In the dim light of the room it seemed to be bluish-black in colour. The man picked up the wooden hammer lying beside it and struck it twice. Then rising, he went out into the corridor and walked off into the inner recesses of the temple. This time the footsteps sounded fainter and fainter as they moved away from the room. Then abruptly they stopped. The sudden silence gave Sosuke a start. He tried to imagine what might now be happening to the man. But the interior of the temple was shrouded in silence. Of the men sitting with him, not one moved so much as a muscle of his face. Sosuke sat waiting for some further sound from the depths of the temple. Then once again a gong shattered the silence, and once again he heard footsteps in the long corridor, approaching the room. The man in the *hakama* appeared and, still in silence, passed through the room and out of the door, and vanished into the cold outside. Then another man rose and struck the gong as before. He too could be heard walking down the corridor into the depths of the temple. As he observed this procession in silence, Sosuke sat with his hands on his knees, waiting for his turn to come.

Shortly after the man next but one to him left the room, a loud cry was heard from within. Since it came from far away, it did not strike Sosuke's eardrums with so great a force, but he could tell that whoever it was had put all of himself into the cry, and that it had definitely come from just one throat. When the man next to him rose, he knew that his turn was finally at hand, and he lost even more of his self-possession.

Sosuke had prepared some kind of anwer to the *koan* that had been given him, but it was a very shabby answer. Since he couldn't get by without saying something when he entered the *roshi*'s room, he had been forced to seize upon some kind of makeshift solution to the problem he had been unable to solve, a solution devised solely for this one interview. He was not under the slightest illusion that he would be able to cut through his Gordian knot with this makeshift answer. He had no intention, of course, of trying to deceive the *roshi*. Sosuke was too serious about this experiment to attempt such a thing. Feeling himself under an obligation to go in to see the *roshi*, he was ashamed of his own emptiness as he took in with him only something devised in his head, a thing of absolutely no value.

He struck the gong as he had seen the others do. But even as he did so, he realized that he did not have the same right as the others to be striking the gong with the hammer. He felt a deep self-contempt as monkey-like he imitated the others.

Filled with fear for this self that was so weak, he left the room and set foot in the cold corridor. The corridor was long, and the rooms to the right were all dark. Turning round two corners, he saw light behind the *shoji* of a room at the corridor's end. He walked to the entrance of the room and stopped.

It was proper etiquette for the man entering to do reverence three times to the *roshi*. The reverence was to be done by squatting and bending the head all the way down to the *tatami*, at the same time bringing both hands with palms upward up to the ears, as if they were holding something. Sosuke knelt on the threshold and performed the prescribed reverence.

'Once is enough,' said a voice within. Sosuke rose and entered.

The room was illuminated only by a dim light, so dim, in fact, that even writing in relatively large characters would not have been decipherable. In all his experience Sosuke had never met anyone who entertained the night with so faint a light. It was, of course, stronger than moonlight and lacked the moon's bluish tinge, but it gave the illusion that it would recede shortly into total blackness.

In this quiet, indistinct light Sosuke made out four or five feet ahead of him the figure of the man whom Gido called *roshi*. As before, the face was immobile; it might as well have been cast in metal. It was the colour of copper. The *roshi* was dressed in a robe nearly the colour of a persimmon. Neither his hands nor his feet were visible; only his head could be seen. From the neck up, the head gave the impression of relaxation, even in its solemn and rigorous self-control. There was a fascination in knowing that there was no fear of that head's moving, no matter how long he might wait for it to do so. On the scalp, not a single hair was to be seen.

The *roshi* spoke only one sentence to Sosuke, who sat before him, drained of all spirit. 'If you haven't more to offer than that, you shouldn't have come; anyone with even a little education could say as much as you said.'

Sosuke left the room feeling like a dog whose master has died. Behind him the gong clanged loudly.

XX

Sosuke heard someone on the other side of the *shoji* call, 'Mr Nonaka, Mr Nonaka.' Half-waking, he thought he had responded to the call, but actually he lost consciousness and fell sound asleep again before he could make an answer.

When his eyes finally opened, he jumped up in surprise. Going out to the veranda, he found Gido, with a kind of apron over his robe, wiping down the floor. While wringing out his wet rag with hands red and numb from the cold, he greeted Sosuke with his usual gentle, smiling face.

This morning too Gido had already been to the main temple and finished his meditation before coming home and setting about his work. Sosuke was thoroughly embarrassed as he reflected on his sloth in not getting up even after he had been called.

'I'm sorry that I overslept again this morning.'

He slipped hurriedly out of the kitchen door to the well, where he drew the cold water and washed his face as quickly as possible. He stroked with his hands the beard that had grown on his cheeks. It felt rough, but he did not have time to worry about that now. He could not get out of his mind the contrast between Gido and himself.

The day he had received the letter of introduction, Sosuke had been told that the monk, Gido, was a very good man who had already made much progress in the Way. But he hadn't expected to find him as courteous and unassuming as an unlettered servant. To see him working like this with an apron over his robe, no one would have taken him for the master of an independent hermitage. He looked more like an acolyte or an aspirant.

This young priest had come to the temple to do *zazen* when he was still in the world. For seven whole days he had sat in the full lotus position without moving. Finally, his legs were in such pain that he could hardly stand up. When he had to relieve himself, it was all he could do to move his body along the wall. Gido was at that time an architect. The day he achieved enlightenment he ran up the mountain behind the temple in an excess of joy and shouted out in a loud voice, 'Grass, trees, animals, men — everything is Buddha!' And he shaved his head.

Although this hermitage had been entrusted to him for two years already, he had not in all that time, according to his own account, once enjoyed the comfort of sleeping in a relaxed position. Even in winter he slept sitting down, leaning against the wall fully clothed. He told Sosuke that when he was still an acolyte he was made to wash the *roshi*'s underwear. Moreover, when he could steal a little time from his duties to do *zazen*, he would be approached from behind, harangued ill-naturedly in the most abusive language and asked how he had ever managed to become a monk.

'Of late it's finally become a little easier. But there's still the future. The ascetical life of the Way is really a very painful one. If it were easy even a fool like me wouldn't have to spend ten or twenty years in such suffering.'

Sosuke merely stared vacantly ahead. He was impatient with his own lack of endurance and power. But at the same time, if *satori* took so many years to achieve, then why had he come to the mountain to start with? This had been the first contradiction.

'You needn't fear that coming has been a loss. If you sit only ten minutes, you will get ten minutes value from your sitting, and if twenty minutes, twenty. Besides, if you succeed in making the initial breakthrough, you can continue your practice even without remaining here.'

Sosuke had to return to his room and take up his sitting again, if only out of a sense of obligation to Gido.

He was still trying to meditate when Gido came and said, 'Mr Nonaka, it's time for the sermon.' No words could have given him greater pleasure at that moment. Plagued by this difficult conundrum which he could no more grip than a completely bald head, he was finding it excruciating to sit like this in anguish. Any physical labour, however exhausting, would be preferable. What he wanted most was to exercise his body.

The Sermon Hall was about one hundred yards away from the hermitage. They passed again in front of the lotus pond and went straight ahead this time, without turning left, until they came to the end of the lane. There a tall building rose majestically before them among the pines. Gido had the book with the black cover in his pocket. Sosuke was, of course, empty-handed. Not until he had come here did he even know that a sermon was nothing more than a lecture such as he had attended at school.

The room had a high ceiling and was both spacious and cold. The faded colour of the *tatami* met the colour of the ancient pillars to give the room a musty look that told of ages past. The people sitting in the room also seemed sober and subdued. Each sat where he pleased, but there was not one who laughed or even spoke above a whisper. The priests all wore dark blue robes of hemp and sat in front seats facing each other. The seats were painted vermilion.

Finally the *roshi* made his appearance. Sosuke, who kept his eyes fixed on the *tatami*, did not know from which entrance he had come into the room. He caught sight of him for the first time when he was already seated serenely in his chair, which gave him still further dignity. He saw a young priest stand, unfold a dark purple crepe wrapper, and draw from it a manuscript, which he reverently placed on the table before the *roshi*. Then he saw him make a deep bow and retire.

All the monks in the hall brought their hands together in the sign of reverence and began to intone the Counsels of Musokokushi. The other laymen who had taken places around Sosuke also joined in the singing. To Sosuke it sounded half like a sutra and half like ordinary words which had been given a musical notation.

'I have three classes of disciples. The first class, the pro-

199

ficients, are those who in their fervour have broken completely with the outside world and its pursuits and are giving themselves heart and soul to that which concerns them most. The second class consists of those who are not so earnest in their pursuit of the Way and are distracted into intellectual sidepaths' and so forth. The passage chanted was rather short. Sosuke had not known before who Musokokushi was, but from Gido he had heard that Musokokushi and Daitokokushi were the founders of the Rinzai branch of Zen. He had also heard from him that Daitokokushi had been lame and irritated by the fact that he could not fold his legs as he wished. When he was on the point of death, he declared that he would now, at least, do as he desired, and he forced his bad leg into the full lotus position, with the result that blood burst forth and stained his robe.

At length the sermon began. Gido brought his book out of his pocket, opened it at about the middle, and placed it in front of Sosuke. The title of the book was *Shumon mujinto-ron*. When Sosuke had first asked him about it, Gido had said that it was a very helpful and fine book. It was edited by Torei, the disciple of Hakuin, and it summarized in an orderly fashion the stages a man practising Zen must pass through, from the most shallow to the most profound, and described the psychological states accompanying each stage.

Sosuke, who was entering in the middle of the series of sermons, could not understand much that was said; but the *roshi* spoke with eloquence, and as he listened, Sosuke heard many interesting things. It is usual in these sermons to encourage the aspirants to greater effort by introducing examples from the lives of men who have followed the Way with great effort and pain, thus bringing home the points of the sermon. Today also the same method was followed. But at a certain point the *roshi* suddenly changed his tone

200

of voice and began to excoriate the lack of fervour of some of the aspirants before him.

'These days there are those, even among us, who seek to excuse their indolence by pretending fear of delusions.'

These words gave Sosupke quite a shock. For he himself had voiced that very doubt.

One hour later Gido and Sosuke returned together to the hermitage. Gido remarked on the way, 'At these sessions the faults of the aspirants are often denounced in that manner.' Sosuke made no answer.

XXI

The days on the mountain passed one by one. Sosuke had received two rather lengthy letters from Oyone. There was nothing in them, of course, to disturb him or to distract him from his purpose. Though he was ordinarily so thoughtful of his wife, he neglected to answer them. He felt that unless he found an answer to the problem posed to him by the *roshi*, his coming to the mountain would have been in vain. He also felt some compunction towards Gido. In his waking hours he was constantly under a pressure that he could not easily define. As sun after sun rose and set, and his days at the temple accumulated, his inner turmoil mounted and he felt just as if some dread thing were pursuing him. Still, he could only repeat the answer he had given at the first; he knew no way of approaching any nearer to a solution. The more he thought about it, the more firmly he believed in the correctness of his original answer. Since, however, it had been an answer from the head, it had absolutely no value. He tried to put aside this one certainty and search for another, but so far he had been totally unsuccessful.

He sat alone in his room deep in thought. When he got tired, he left the house by the kitchen door, walked out to the vegetable garden at the back, and entered the cave at the foot of the cliff. There he stood absolutely motionless. Gido had told him that he must not allow himself to be distracted, that he should concentrate until he froze and became as hard as iron. The more he heard this repeated, the more difficult it seemed to achieve.

'The trouble with you is that you already have a pre-conceived idea in your head,' Gido warned him again. Sosuke was finally at his wits' end. Suddenly his thoughts turned to Yasui. If it happened that he became a regular visitor at Sakai's and did not return to Manchuria for some time, then it would be wisest for them to abandon their present house immediately and move elsewhere. Rather than waste his time here at the temple, it would be more practical to return to Tokyo at once and look into this. If he did not move quickly, Oyone might learn of Yasui's presence, and this would only increase her worry.

'There doesn't seem to be much chance of anyone like me ever reaching *satori*,' Sosuke, discouraged, announced to Gido one day. This was just two or three days before he actually left the mountain.

'Not at all. Anyone determined to reach *satori* can do so,' Gido answered with conviction. 'You've got to pit yourself full force against the taut strength of the Lotus Sutra, just as if you were beating a drum. When you have become saturated from head to foot with the *koan*, a new heaven and a new earth will suddenly open up before your eyes.'

Sosuke felt a deep sadness that neither by circumstance nor by temperament was he suited to plunge blindly into so desperate a venture. It went without saying that his days at this mountain retreat were numbered. He was a poor fool who had come here with the sole intention of cutting himself loose from the entangling complications of his daily life, and had wound up instead lost and confused in a detour on this mountain.

He lacked the courage to reveal to Gido his true senti-ments. From the bottom of his heart he respected the

202

courage, fervour, earnestness, and kind heart of this young priest.

'There is a saying that though the Way is close at hand, many go far off in search of it. That saying is true. It is right there before your nose, if you would only open your eyes to it,' Gido said regretfully. Sosuke returned to his room and lit another incense stick.

Sosuke continued in this same condition, unfortunately, until the day he had to leave the mountain. He was finally unable to find the opportunity to launch himself forward on a strikingly new course of life. Then it was the morning of departure, and he manfully threw off whatever regrets he felt in leaving.

'Thank you for all you have done. I'm sorry that it was to no avail. I don't suppose I'll have a chance to see you again for quite some time. Take good care of yourself,' Sosuke said to Gido as he prepared to depart.

Gido seemed to be feeling sorry for him as he answered, 'I'm afraid I've been of no help whatsoever. On the contrary, you must have found this place extremely inconvenient and uncomfortable. Still, having done even this much *zazen* will make quite a difference in your life. It's already much that you should have come here like this.'

Despite the reassurance, Sosuke saw clearly that it had all been a waste of time. He felt ashamed to have Gido try to put a face on his failure like this.

'Whether *satori* comes early or late depends on a person's temperament. It has nothing to do with his character or lack of it. Also, it sometimes happens that a *satori* too easily achieved later becomes obstructed, and one reached only after long arduous efforts becomes the source of a very deep and lasting pleasure and satisfaction. There's no reason to give up hope. But ardour is necessary. There are men like the late Kosen, who was originally a follower of Confucius and began to practise *zazen* only in middle life. The first three years after becoming a monk, he was unable to solve a single *koan*. He was convinced that he was too sinful ever to reach *satori*. He felt himself lower than dung. Yet look at the enlightenment he finally achieved! He is an excellent example.'

Gido seemed to wish to warn Sosuke indirectly that he should not despair of *satori* even after he returned to Tokyo. Sosuke listened politely to what he said, but in his heart he felt it was no longer a matter of great importance whether he ever reached *satori* or not. He had come here to have the gate opened to him, but its warden had remained obstinately within, and had not so much as shown his face, however long he knocked. The only greeting he had received was, 'It's no use knocking. Open the gate yourself and enter.' He had thought and thought how he might unbolt the gate, and he had formulated a clear plan in his head. But he had been incapable finally of developing in himself the power to achieve his purpose. He was standing now in exactly the same spot in which he had stood before he had even begun to search for a solution. He was left standing before the closed door, ignorant and impotent. Through the years he had relied solely upon his own powers of discretion. It was cruelly ironic that it should be this very self-reliant discretion that had proved to be a curse to him now. In his present mood he envied the unsubtle simplicity of the fool, who follows a course of action without having to weigh the possibilities or puzzle over the means; and he looked with near reverence upon the dedication of the simple good men and women who were firmly anchored in their beliefs and undisturbed by intellectual doubts. It seemed to him that he had been fated from birth to stand forever outside the gate, unable to pass through. There was nothing he could do about it. But if the gate were really impassable, then it had been a contradiction to come here in the first place. He looked behind him and he lacked the courage to retrace his steps along the road he had come. He looked ahead at the firmly-bolted door that would never open to reveal the view beyond. He was not a man, then, to pass through, nor was he yet one who could be content to remain on the outside. In short, he was a poor unfortunate doomed to squat before the gate waiting for night to fall.

Before departing, Sosuke went with Gido to take his leave of the *roshi*. The *roshi* led them to the room with the banistered veranda overlooking the lotus pond. Gido, without being asked, poured tea and then left the two alone.

'Tokyo is probably still quite cold,' began the *roshi*. 'If only you had been able to get even a slight hold, it would have been easier when you got home. I'm sorry.'

Sosuke responded to the *roshi's* words with a polite bow. Then he went out of the temple gate that he had first entered ten days earlier. Behind him the cryptomeria trees bore down upon the roof-tiles of the temple and soared black to the sky, sealing in winter.

XXII

The Sosuke that crossed the threshold of his own house again cut a sad figure indeed, even to his own eyes. For the past ten days he had merely doused his head in cold water upon rising and had not taken a comb to his hair in all that time. It was long since he had had time to shave. Thanks to the solicitous care of Gido, he had eaten cooked rice three times a day, but all he had had with it were boiled herbs or boiled radish. His face was always naturally pale, but now it looked even more haggard than on the day he had left. Moreover, he had become accustomed at the hermitage to giving himself to deep and prolonged thought, and something of this remained with him still. Oyone was reminded of a hen brooding over her eggs. He was not as alert as he had been before. Nevertheless, he had Sakai on his mind, or rather, Sakai's brother, whom he had heard called an adventurer, and Yasui, the very mention of whose name as a friend of the brother had caused him such consternation. He was anxious to get further news about them, but he lacked the courage to go himself to the landlord's house and inquire. Nor, with still better reason, could he ask about them indirectly through Oyone. So afraid was he that she might find out about Yasui that there had not been a single day on the mountain that he had not prayed that no word of Yasui's presence in Tokyo would leak out to her. Sosuke sat down in his own familiar parlour.

'I wonder why it is that even a short train ride can be so tiring. Only imagination, perhaps. Did anything come up while I was away?' His face did, in fact, look fatigued even after the short trip from Kamakura.

No matter what might happen, Oyone never forgot to present to her husband a smiling face, but now, in her sympathy for him, it was more than she could manage. Still, she could not tell him directly, just after he had returned from the place where he had gone to rest, that he looked worse than before he had set out.

She feigned a sprightliness she did not feel as she said, 'Even after a good rest, it's natural to feel a bit let down on coming home. But you look like a tramp. For goodness sake, take a short nap, then go to the bath. Also, get a haircut and a shave.' She took a little mirror from a drawer in the desk and let him see what he looked like.

Listening to his wife fuss over him, Sosuke felt as if the air of the hermitage was finally being blown away. Now that he had left the mountain and returned home, he was his old self again.

'Did you get any word from Sakai in my absence?'

'No, nothing.'

'Not even about Koroku?'

'No.'

Koroku had gone to the library. Sosuke left the house with towel and soap in hand.

206

When Sosuke went to the office the next day, everyone inquired about his health. Some even mentioned that he seemed to have lost weight. This sounded to Sosuke like subtle sarcasm. The man who read *Saikontan* merely asked how things had gone. Sosuke was quite pained by this question too.

That evening he had to undergo another round of questioning from Oyone and Koroku, who in turns inquired about even minute details.

'It must be very nice,' remarked Oyone, 'to be able to go out without having to worry about someone to watch over the house.'

'How much do they charge a day?' asked Koroku. 'It would be fun to go there with a rifle and do some hunting.'

'But it must have been boring . . . to stay in such a lonely place. You can't spend all your time sleeping,' added Oyone.

'But without more nourishing food, it can't be very good for the health.' This from Koroku.

After he had gone to bed, Sosuke determined to go the following day to Sakai's and inquire directly about Yasui. If the latter were still in Tokyo and there was likelihood that his visits to Sakai would continue, Sosuke was resolved to leave their present home and move far away.

Next morning the sun rose upon an ordinary day for Sosuke, and sank again into the west, uneventfully. In the evening he told Oyone he was just going to run up to Sakai's for a moment and he went out of the gate. There was no moon as he climbed the hill. He entered Sakai's yard from the side gate. The sound of his feet on the gravel path, illuminated by a gas lamp, broke the silence of the night. He screwed up his courage and determined that there was little chance of encountering Yasui at Sakai's that evening. All the same, he took the precaution of going to the kitchen entrance and inquiring first if there were guests in the house.

207

'I'm glad you came. It's still as cold as ever, isn't it?' said Sakai on seeing him. Full of life as always, he had a large number of children lined up before him and he was playing a game of *janken* with one. His adversary was a little girl of about six, who wore on her head a wide red ribbon tied to look like a butterfly. Not to be outdone by Sakai, she clenched her small fist tightly and thrust it out with great energy. Her look of determination and the contrast between her tiny fist and Sakai's huge one was making everybody laugh.

'This time it's Yukiko's turn to win,' said Mrs Sakai, watching the game from her place beside the brazier. She showed her teeth in a pleasant smile. Around the children lay strewn beads of all colours, white, red, indigo, and so on.

'Finally I've lost to Yukiko,' said Sakai, leaving the game and coming toward Sosuke. 'Can I drag you to my den again tonight?'

On the pillar in the study still hung the Mongolian sword enclosed in the brocaded bag. For flower arrangement there were yellow *sai*. Sosuke wondered where they might be in bloom this early in the year. His eyes rose to the colourful brocaded bag, hanging half-way up the pillar of the *tokonoma*, and he said, 'I see it's still hanging there,' looking at the same time for Sakai's reaction.

'Yes, but this Mongolian sword is a little bit too much of a curiosity, isn't it? My no-good brother thinks that by giving me a toy like this he can wheedle what he wants out of me.'

'What's happened to your brother since I saw you last?' Sosuke tried to appear unconcerned.

'He finally returned to Mongolia four or five days ago. He's just made for the place. When I told him that a barbarian such as he would be a misfit in Tokyo and that he should go back quickly to Mongolia, he agreed and returned. I'm convinced that he's a man who should remain on the other side of the Great Wall, or who should be looking for diamonds in the Gobi Desert.'

'What about his companion?'

'Yasui? He went back with him, of course. He's a man who just doesn't seem to be able to settle down to anything. I've heard that he was once a student at Kyoto University. I wonder what caused him to change so completely?'

Sosuke felt perspiration under his armpits. It was painful to hear how Yasui had changed and how unsettled he was. He only thanked heaven that he had never mentioned to Sakai that he too had been a student at the same university Yasui had attended. Still, he was the man that Sakai had proposed to introduce to his brother and Yasui on the day when he had invited these two to dinner. Although he had narrowly escaped the embarrassment of showing his face there that night, it was not impossible that his name had come up in the conversation. Sosuke understood why people with shady pasts found it convenient to adopt an alias in facing the world. It was all he could do to restrain himself from coming out openly and asking Sakai, 'You didn't by any chance happen to bring up my name in front of Yasui?' But that was the one thing he must not do.

The maid entered with a large flat cake tray heaped with unusual cakes. They were about the size of a square of *tofu* and made of a kind of transparent gelatin. Two little goldfish could be seen at the centre of each. They had been carefully transferred on to the cake-plate without destroying their shape. Sosuke looked at the cakes and thought them quaint, but his attention was turned in quite another direction.

'Please go ahead,' said Sakai, as he himself began to eat the cakes. 'I was given these at a silver wedding anniversary yesterday. Since they are a present, it's good luck to eat them. I'm sure you can use a bit of good luck yourself.'

Under this pretext, Sakai managed to dispose of several of the very sweet cakes. He was a man of exuberantly good

209

health who could drink sake and tea, and eat rice and cakes as he wished.

'The fact is, however, I fail to see why it should be considered so auspicious for a man and a woman to become full of wrinkles living with each other for twenty or thirty years. I suppose it's all relative. I remember passing by Shimizudani Park once and being surprised.' The conversation had taken a strange turn. Going in this way from one subject to another without giving his guest a chance to get bored was a usual technique of Sakai, skilled as he was in social intercourse.

According to Sakai's account, in early spring, countless frogs are born in the narrow, sewer-like stream that flows under Benkei Bridge and into Shimizudani Park. As they grow up amidst much jostling and crying, hundreds, even thousands of couples form and mate in the water of the stream. These mating couples cover the stream from the park all the way to the bridge, with not an opening anywhere. As they float there in this conjugal harmony, passers-by — shop apprentices, men of leisure, and such — throw stones at them and cruelly kill the mating frogs. The number of couples thus killed is almost beyond count.

'The expression "piles of corpses" certainly applies here. And these are all couples, which makes it all the sadder. So you see, just in walking a few blocks, one never knows how many tragedies one may encounter. Considering this, I think we can account ourselves lucky. There is no danger that anyone will tell us that there's anything wrong in being man and wife, and knock off our heads with stones. And if the two have really lived twenty or thirty years together uneventfully, then they are undoubtedly to be congratulated. So I guess the least we can do is eat their cakes.' Saying this, Sakai took up another cake with his chopsticks and placed it before Sosuke, who received it with a forced smile.

Sakai told these half-facetious stories one after the other, and Sosuke, in spite of himself, found interest in the conversation to a point, but at the bottom of his heart he could never give himself to this kind of banter like Sakai. Finally he excused himself and left the house. When he looked up at the still moonless sky, he discovered in its deep darkness a kind of sad grandeur that was beyond description.

He had gone to Sakai's only in the hope of finding that all might still be well. To establish this, he had put aside all shame and fastidiousness and had skilfully manoeuvred his conversation with this gentleman, who was so full of honesty and benevolence. Even if he had not learned all that he wished to learn, he had not had the courage nor had he been faced with the necessity to reveal a word about his past.

The thunderstorm that had threatened to burst over his head had passed by, leaving him unscathed. But he had the presentiment that he would have to confront many similar occasions for worry in the future. It would be heaven that would prepare each such confrontation, and it would be he that would have to do his best to escape each time.

XXIII

With the beginning of the new month it became very much warmer. The weeding-out of public office employees in connection with the imminent rise in salaries, which had been the subject of speculation for so long, had been accomplished by the end of the old month. While it was taking place, Sosuke would hear of this man or that being fired — some he knew and some he didn't — and he would say to Oyone, 'I guess I'm next.' Oyone could not tell if he were joking or serious. At times his words sounded to her like an ill augur of the still hidden future, and even Sosuke, who had pronounced them, felt a cloud pass over his heart.

But when the new month arrived and he knew that the upheaval at the office was over, at least for the present,

Sosuke thought deeply about his fate in having survived. While survival seemed natural enough to him from one point of view, still — from another angle — it seemed merely a stroke of chance. He stood looking down at Oyone and said with great gravity, 'I made it.' He seemed neither happy nor sad about it. In fact, at that moment he looked to Oyone like a clown fallen from the sky.

Two or three days later Sosuke's salary went up five yen. 'It's not a 2.5 per cent increase as expected, but that can't be helped. I'm better off than the ones who lost their jobs, and even of those who remained there are many who got no increase at all.' Sosuke seemed contented, as if the five-yen rise were more than he deserved. Oyone could not, of course, find it in her heart to complain against such treatment.

Next evening at dinner Sosuke found on his tray a large fish complete with head and with a tail that extended beyond the plate, and rice with red azuki-bean mixed in, giving it colour. Oyone had sent Kiyo to invite Koroku, who had already moved in with Sakai.

Koroku entered from the kitchen, and when he saw the table exclaimed, 'You've prepared a real feast!'

Then it was the season when plum blossoms met the eye here and there. The earliest flowers, in fact, had already lost their colour and begun to fall. Rain too fell gently like a mist. And when the rain stopped and the sun came out, the days were hot and sultry. From the ground and from the rooftops rose a humidity that could not but call forth memories of springs past. There were days too when puppies frolicked about the umbrellas opened out to dry near the back door, and when heat waves could be seen flowing from the parts of the umbrellas that caught the sun.

'Winter has finally fled. Why don't you go over to the Saekis next Saturday and see what to do about Koroku? If you wait too long, Yasu will forget again,' Oyone urged Sosuke.

'Yes, I'll go next Saturday,' he answered with determination.

Koroku had accepted Sakai's offer to live at his place and help out around the house. Sosuke had then proposed to Koroku that he, Sosuke, and Yasunosuke should provide what he still lacked. Koroku had not waited for any other move on Sosuke's part but had gone directly to talk to Yasunosuke on his own. He returned with Yasunosuke's promise that if Sosuke were to make an appeal to him, he would accept immediately his share of the burden of Koroku's school expenses, thus settling the matter.

In this way peace descended upon the couple who had such a disaste for complications. One Sunday morning Sosuke went to the local bath to wash off a four-day accumulation of grime. There he overheard a man of about fifty with close-shaven head, obviously a Buddhist priest, greet another in his thirties, who had the look of a merchant, by commenting that spring had finally arrived. The younger man remarked that that very morning he had heard for the first time the song of the bush warbler. The older answered that he himself had heard one already two or three days before.

'It's still the beginning of the season, so he wasn't in very good voice.'

'Yes, his tongue is still thick.'

When Sosuke got home, he recounted to Oyone the conversation he had overheard at the bath. Oyone, looking out from the glass window of the *shoji* at the bright scene that lay before her, remarked, with cheerful face,

'It's a good thing, isn't it. Spring is finally here.'

Sosuke stepped on to the veranda and began to clip his finger nails, which had grown to quite a length.

'But it will soon be winter again,' he said, as with downcast eyes he continued to cut his nails.

GLOSSARY

amado   wooden shutters that slide into place

bakufu   the Japanese feudal government under the Shogun

basho   banana plant, *Musa paradisiaca*

chanoma   small sitting-room, not as large as the parlour

geta   wooden clogs

gidayu   a form of ballad-drama

hagi   bush clover, *Lespedeza*

hakama   a kind of divided skirt worn by men on formal occasions

haori   Japanese coat, half-length, worn with the *kimono*

Hekiganshu   a collection of koan with annotations, compiled in 1125

janken   the game known in the West as 'Scissors, paper, stone'

joruri   a ballad-drama, such as those composed by Chikamatsu Monzaemon (1653-1725)

kakemono   a hanging picture or scroll, displayed usually in the *tokonoma*

kikyo   Chinese balloon flower, *Platycodon grandiflorium*

Korai   a type of china that was made in Korea in the Korai age (from the beginning of the tenth century to the end of the fourteenth century)

kotatsu   contraption for keeping warm. Hot coals are placed under a table which is then covered with a quilt to keep in the heat

kuzu   arrowroot, *Pueraria*

manju   a bun with bean-jam stuffing

misoshiru   soup made of bean paste, commonly served at breakfast

moso   a species of bamboo, *Phyllostachys mitis*

Nanshu   a style of painting associated with the Chinese Southern Zen school of the twelfth and thirteenth centuries

natto   fermented soybeans

nemaki   an unlined cotton garment worn for sleeping

obi   sash worn with the *kimono* and *yukata,* by both men and women

ominaeshi   Patrinia scabiosae folia

rin   the smallest denomination of Japanese currency

sai   hilum

Saikontan   an epigrammatic prose poem combining elements of Confucianism, Taoism and Buddhism, written by Kojisei. Details of the life of the author and the date of the book are not known, but it was already in existence in 1624

shoji   sliding-doors made of paper

soba   buckwheat vermicelli

sumi-e   charcoal sketches

susuki   Japanese pampas grass, *Miscanthus Sinensis*

tabi   Japanese footwear somewhat resembling socks

tatami   mats used on the floor of Japanese homes

tofu   bean-curds, a common item in the Japanese diet

tokonoma   the recess in a Japanese room in which pictures are hung and flower arrangements displayed

tsuta   Japanese ivy, *Parthenocissus tricuspidata*

urajiro   whitebeam, *Gleichenia*

yose   a Japanese variety show

yukata   an unlined cotton garment, worn by both men and women, which resembles a *kimono*

yuzuri   Daphniphyllum macropodum

Zenkan sakushin   a work on Zen written by the Chinese monk of Unseiji temple, Chuko, during the Ming period

zoni   a soup containing rice cakes and vegetables, a common item on the New Year's Day menu

zori   a special kind of sandal

SELECT BIOGRAPHIES

Ganku (1749-1838), a Japanese painter.

Gantai (1782-1865), a Japanese painter, son of Ganku.

Hakuin (1685-1768), a priest of the Rinzai sect of Zen. He became a monk of Shinshu Buddhism. He painted in the style of Sotatsu.

Ito Hirobumi (1841-1909), Japanese statesman who played a leading role in the making of modern Japan. He was assassinated on 26 October, 1909, during a visit to Harbin in Manchuria.

Hoitsu (1761-1828), brother of the lord of the Himeji Castle, Sakai Tadasane.

Watanabe Kazan (1793-1841), a Japanese painter.

Kiichi (1796-1858), a Japanese poet whose real name was Suzuki Motonaga.

Musokokushi (1275-1351), a priest of the Rinzai sect of Zen.

Sodehagi, a character appearing in Chikamatsu's play, *Okushu Adachihara*.

Sokui, a Chinese monk of the Obaku sect of Zen who came to Japan with Ingen in 1654.

Torei (1721-92), a priest of the Rinzai sect of Zen.

ABOUT THE AUTHOR

Natsume Soseki, one of Japan's most distinguished writers, was born in Tokyo in 1867. At an early age he studied the Chinese classics, and though later intending to become an architect, he changed his mind, and entered Tokyo Imperial University to take up literature. In 1900 he was sent to London by the Japanese Ministry of Education to study English literature for two years. On his return he was appointed lecturer in English at Tokyo University. After publishing his first novel, *I Am a Cat*, in 1905, he immediately rose to fame. Shortly after this he resigned his post at the university to become literary editor of the Asahi newspaper. Many more novels followed, and Soseki became the leading voice of the age, often ruthlessly criticizing his contemporary society for its acceptance of westernization. He died in 1916 at the age of forty-nine.